ONCE UPON
A TIME
IT WAS NOW

JAMES ALEXANDER THOM
Author of *Follow the River*

BLUE RIVER PRESS
Indianapolis, Indiana

Once Upon a Time It Was Now

The Art and Craft of Writing Historical Fiction, Second Edition

Copyright © 2010, 2017 by James Alexander Thom

Published by **Blue River Press**
Indianapolis, Indiana
www.brpressbooks.com

Distributed by **Cardinal Publishers Group**
Tom Doherty Company, Inc.
www.cardinalpub.com

ISBN: 978-1-68157-051-8

Cover Design: Scott Lohr
Cover Photo: Marzolino / Shutterstock.com
Editor: Dani McCormick
Printed in the United States of America
23 22 21 20 19 18 17   1 2 3 4 5

DEDICATION

To Sister Julie

TABLE OF CONTENTS

Preface

ONCE UPON A TIME
IT WAS NOW

They got married and lived happily ever after.

There! I've always wanted to start a book at that end. And I'll finish it:

Once upon a time.

I certainly can do that: play with time, switch a story end-to-end, see the past and the future simultaneously, predict yesterday and forget tomorrow.

Having spent most of my career as a historical novelist, I've developed godlike powers over the dimension of time. That is, godlike as in Janus, the Roman god with one face looking forward, the other backward. January, the doorway between last year and next, is named after Janus. To me, Janus is the personification of historical perception.

Janus-like, I might write: *They will live happily ever after ... until the divorce.*

For, you see, a career spent writing in historical time about real people and events has convinced me that there are more happy beginnings than happy endings. But, happy endings aren't as essential to good storytelling as most people think. Stories with unhappy endings can teach and inspire just as well as those ending "happily ever after." And usually they work better, because they're more true to life.

In this book, I will compare historical novelists with historians. The two are much alike; both tell stories of the past. But the historian's viewpoint faces backward only. He is limited to looking back in time; the historical novelist is not. Limited only by imagination, a historical novelist can go wild with time, just as wild as any science-fiction writer.

For example, one day, long ago, I picked up a science-fiction book that began, "Once upon a time, there will be ...." And it went on from there to tell a story set in the future. That was a delightfully playful opening, and an understandable sentence — like something the god Janus might say. At the time, I wished I'd thought of it.

In my long career in this historical fiction business, though, I've found that the most effective storytelling concept is this:

Once upon a time it was now.

That has become my credo and my method as a longtime historical novelist. It's quite simple, if you see as Janus sees:

Today is now.

Yesterday was now.

Tomorrow will be now.

Three hundred years ago, the eighteenth century was now.

You, as a historical novelist, can make any time now by taking your reader into that time. Once you grasp that, the rest is just hard work.

Stay with me, and you'll see how such work is done.

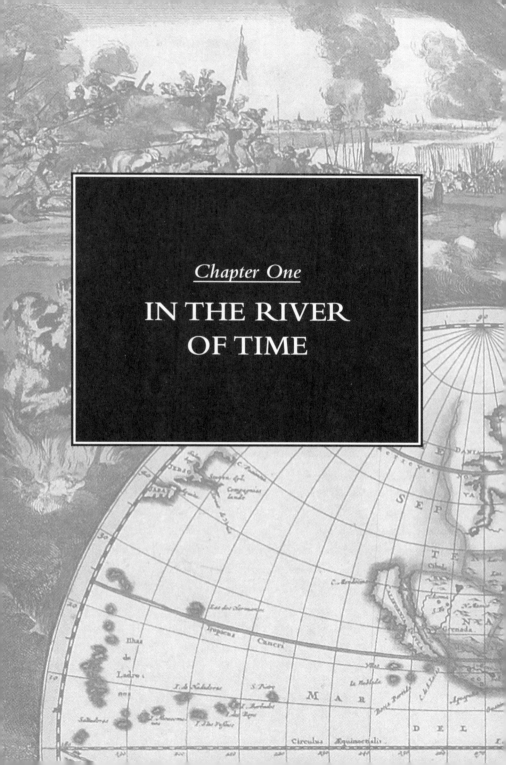

Chapter One

IN THE RIVER
OF TIME

nce upon a time, just a few months ago (a time we then thought of as "now"), the mother of a teenage girl lamented to me that her daughter simply was not interested in history. Not through school, History Channel programs, movies, old photo albums, or even the most earnest family conversations could the girl be roused to the least level of enthusiasm for anything concerning history.

In exasperation, the mother sat her down and asked her to explain her antipathy toward something as important and fascinating as history. The girl rolled her eyes, sighed, shrugged, and finally exclaimed: "Because I'm not in it!"

What a telling statement! Of course! Not only is history taught in dull ways, full of dates and meaningless names and places she's expected to remember and might be tested on, it's utterly irrelevant to her because she hadn't been born yet! She said a mouthful in that explanation.

Or, maybe she meant she wasn't recorded in MySpace or Facebook. Maybe her schoolmates hadn't texted each other calling her a geek or a slut. Maybe that's when history begins for young persons of today: when they are mentioned online.

But she was wrong to believe she's not in history. She didn't understand that she *is* a part of the historical story; she just hasn't yet caught up with the place in the story where she's been born. Her ancestors, or her American forebears who founded the country she now lives in, are the earlier chapters of that same story in which she'll appear soon enough. She is the result of that earlier history, the outcome of those people and what they did. They are part of her.

She and they are all part of the same story. The story of the world, of America, of any community or institution or family, flows like a river, and we are all in it—some of us dead, some old, some young, some as yet unborn. Some of us are upstream; our ancestors are farther downstream; our young or yet unborn descendants still farther upstream. The River of History has countless tributaries and constantly comprises everything that flows into it.

The schoolgirl is in the River of History. She just doesn't feel immersed yet.

UP TO HERE IN HISTORY

Some of us are fortunate enough to feel ourselves immersed in the flow of history from a very young age. Personally, I have always felt that I'm in it, clear up to here.

I'm old enough that I can remember direct ancestors and old relatives who were veterans of the Civil War and the Spanish-American War. I remember their faces and their voices and their smells of tobacco, whiskey, farmyard, liniment, and the plain smell of old working men in the days before people used deodorant. I remember as a small child going to their funerals, their honor guards standing by, frail and white-bearded in their blue Union army uniforms. Such memories connect a child with the river of history, because a family shares the stream of another river: its blood.

My namesake was killed in the Civil War at Fredericksburg. A great grandfather survived the hellish prison camp at Andersonville. His grandson, my father, served in the army in both world wars. Less than ten years after my father returned from the Pacific, I crossed it, going to Korea on a Marine troopship. Bloodlines are another kind of current in the River of Time, and they carry other streams of connection, such as soldiering, or family trades, or religious and political traditions, or fraternal orders and so on. In some families more than in others kinship bonds and behavioral traits are so strong that they're seldom out of mind. Not to mention family feuds. Many families in modern America are still divided by the Civil War.

In some families, storytelling, either proud or rueful of the fore-bears, plays a big role, while there's very little of that in other families. As a child, I knew of our family progression and of the history we'd been through, so I had always been aware of the flow of the river of history through time, and of my place in the flow, upstream from some of us, downstream from others. Unlike that woman's teenage daughter, I never felt that I wasn't a part of history. And when I look at the old photographs of my ancestors, or visit the grave of a Revolutionary War veteran who was our first Thom to come over from Scotland, or read my mother's maiden name in *Moby-Dick*, I know they are all in me.

SHAPING THE PAST

The fortunes of some people, like stockbrokers on Wall Street, lie in something called "futures." The fortunes of others—royalty, for example— lie in the past, by inheritance.

The fortunes (modest though they may be) of historians and historical novelists also lie in the past. The past is where we get the raw materials we use to make the stories by which we earn our bread. The raw material is already there, inexhaustible. We pick bygone time up by the handfuls and, like clay, see if it feels right and then form it into stories about the past.

Of course, it's in the present time that we do this work, and we do it with the intent that someone will publish it and some-one else will read it in the future. We have to function in the present, just as ordinary people do. But the past is what we're us-ing to shape our stories.

Think of it this way: A historical novelist seizes the past and forms a story out of it. A contemporary novelist uses the present. A science-fiction writer might reach forward into the future for the stuff he'll use.

Once we've got our hands on the "stuff," we can play God with it, creating events and characters. You might remember that *Far Side* cartoon by Gary Larsen, in which God is making creatures out of clay. He's rolling the clay between his palms, smiling and thinking, "Snakes are easy!" (Humans, on the other hand, are more complicated.)

How many other occupations let you play God? God created everything by thinking it up. That's what a novelist gets to do, too.

The story of the world, of America, of any community or institution or family, flows like a river, and we are all in it — some of us dead, some old, some young, some as yet unborn.

If you doubt that, look at what I've been doing the last few months with the clay of past time in my hands: I've gone back in time 143 years, to the end of the Civil War, right after President Lincoln's assassination. I've become a war-frazzled, whiskey-loving character named Padraic Quinn, a war correspondent for *Harper's Weekly Magazine*. I've shed forty years to become Quinn, who is thirty-five years old and has just married a beautiful, young woman who he fears outclasses his roguish Irish self. Not only is he beneath her in social standing, he's self-conscious as an amputee, having lost his left hand years before on a battlefield. But his quick, hard Irish right fist is ready to compensate for it, especially if he's had a drink. Quinn doesn't know yet what a good man he is; the test is yet to come. Right in the middle of his New Orleans honeymoon, Quinn gets himself assigned by the magazine to go by steamboat up the Mississippi River to Illinois and cover President Lincoln's final funeral rites in Springfield.

So now, far back in the River of Time, I, as Quinn, am also on a real river, the great Mississippi, on a side-wheeler steamboat heading

WRITING SCHEDULE (HA HA)

During public question and answer sessions, one of the first questions I often get asked is "What's your daily writing schedule like?"

Now, every author has a different answer. Mine, unfortunately, is this: "Which schedule, the ideal or the real?"

THE IDEAL: Rise at daybreak, get coffee, go straight to the desk, write at least a thousand words by lunchtime, and finish another thousand in the afternoon, leaving enough daylight for outdoor chores. Evening is for reading, reviewing research, or making notes on the next day's writing.

THE REAL: Get out of bed by lunchtime (because I didn't get to bed until dawn). Answer voicemail, e-mails and letters, work the New York Times Crossword for mental exercise, talk on the porch or by the fireplace with drop-in visitors, or otherwise procrastinate until the evening news hour. Eat, wash the dinner dishes, spend some quality time with my wife. Now there's no excuse not to go write. Well after midnight, I'll have so much momentum going that I don't quit until I'm worn out.

When I was young, I had prodigious endurance and strict self-discipline. Now I'm way past retirement age and have been working full-time for sixty-five years, so I don't feel guilty about goofing off a little. Besides, I now have a wife who's better company than any typewriter. Old friends merit more attention, too.

But when deadlines loom, I rally, and can work almost around the clock, through pain to numbness, and keep going to the end.

So, the real is far from the ideal. Even when I'm trying to stick to the ideal schedule, of course, I'm susceptible to a condition beyond my control: creative insomnia. If I can't sleep because my mind is at work, I get up and follow it to the typewriter. The Old Gray Matter, she ain't what she used to be, and on those rare occasions when the brain is really functioning, I'd be a fool not to use it.

upstream to cover the saddest story of my career. Within twenty-four hours, this steamboat is going to blow up, killing most of the passengers onboard. I, Quinn, don't know that yet, of course. If I knew it, I'd take my bride and get off the boat here at Vicksburg, or at the next port, Memphis. As the author, though, I know all this already, because it's historical fact, and I've researched it fully. So, with my supernatural novelist's powers, I am two persons at once: Quinn and the novelist who invented him. I am in two different places: my writing office and on a doomed steamboat in the middle of the Mississippi. And I live in two different centuries: the nineteenth and the twenty-first.

As Quinn, I keep a diary and a notebook, all written in cursive script with a pencil or sometimes with a steel-nib pen. As a famous Harper's correspondent, I can telegraph the magazine's New York City office (but only when I'm ashore in a town important enough to have a telegraph line). If I were another famous war correspondent, Ernie Pyle, I'd use a portable typewriter; yet, Pyle, rest his dear departed soul, isn't born yet in Quinn's lifetime and was killed in my own lifetime. Depending on which me is speaking, Pyle's typewriter isn't invented yet, or it's so obsolete I can hardly get a ribbon for it.

And something else that certainly isn't invented yet in Quinn's lifetime is this laptop computer with which I write Quinn's pen and pencil diary entries. How can I write from Quinn's point of view with an instrument that hasn't been invented yet?

Well, it's easy if you're a historical novelist with the superhuman, Janus-like power of being as many different persons as you want to be, in whatever centuries you choose, and in any geographical locations you want to enter and leave. And you know then, as the saying goes, what you know now, even though the character you embody in the story doesn't know it yet. Could

God himself have had more fun with the creative power than this? Wouldn't you like to have this superhuman power?

Read on, then. This book teaches you how to play with time and to do it so well that even a modern American high-school girl, stubbornly impermeable to history, will start reading a story and suddenly feel that she's in it up to her neck; she's even over her head in it, in the flowing River of Time.

And if you write it well enough, that reader might send you the first letter she's ever written to an author, underlining in purple marker the part that says, "I FELT LIKE I WAS THERE!"

As a historical novelist, that's what you want to hear from your readers. Therefore, you must learn all the tricks and techniques to make the reader feel immersed in history. But it's more than just tricks and techniques. It's a sort of transcendental state.

Don't let that scare you, though. Come along.

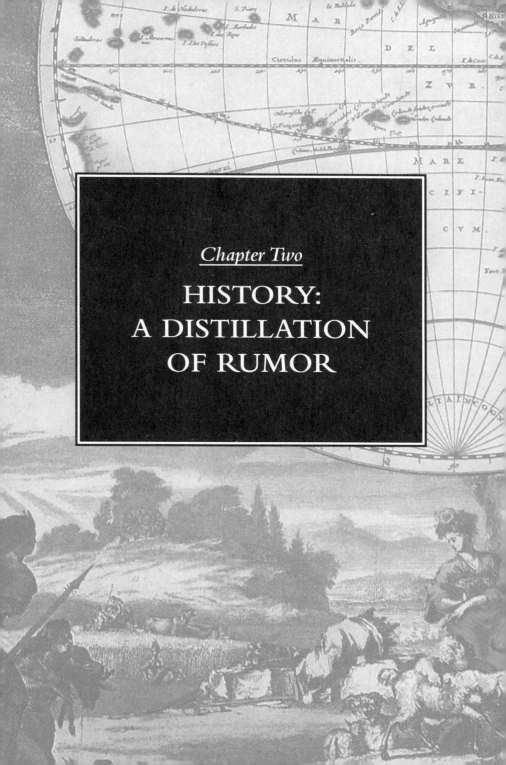

Chapter Two

HISTORY:
A DISTILLATION
OF RUMOR

The world's oldest profession isn't what you might think. Storytelling is older.

In fact, the words *history* and *story* come from the same Latin root and mean almost the same thing. But we've come to think of "history" as stories of times past. History has also become the title of a major subject in school. It's not a particularly popular subject, because students often feel "they're not in it," and because it's such old stuff and often taught in boring rote ways.

And not only is it old but it's said to be the "truth," so we're obliged to know it. But if you know how histories get written, you suspect that the truth of history is often dubious, at best. In fact, the title subject of this book makes me smile and shake my head: *Historical Fiction*. The phrase is redundant. Most history is more fiction than we like to admit.

Most historical accounts were written by fallible scholars, using incomplete or biased resource materials; written through the scholars' own conscious or unconscious predilections; published by textbook or printing companies that have a stake in maintaining a certain set of beliefs; subtly influenced by entities of government and society—national administrations, state education departments, local school boards, etcetera—that also wish to maintain certain sets of beliefs. To be blunt about it, much of the history of many countries and states is based on delusion, propaganda, misinformation, and omission.

It's a problem at least as old as the Athenian historian Thucydides, who qualified his history of the Peloponnesian War by admitting "the want of coincidence between accounts of the same occurrences by different eyewitnesses, arising sometimes from imperfect memory, sometimes from undue partiality for one side or the other."

One of the first lessons I learned as a newspaper reporter long ago was that there will be at least as many descriptions of any simple incident as there are witnesses. Add more versions as time passes and as the eyewitnesses rethink their memories. Apply that lesson to deliberate or motivated events like crimes, battles, love affairs, and public hearings, and you come to understand that history might be, as Thomas Carlyle put it, "a distillation of rumor," or, as Napoleon said, "a set of lies generally agreed upon."

A novel, or so-called "fiction," if deeply researched and conscientiously written, might well contain as much truth as a high-school history textbook approved by a state board of education. But having been designated "historical fiction" by its publisher, it is presumed to be less reliably true than that textbook. If fiction were defined as "the opposite of truth," then much of the content of many approved historical textbooks could be called "historical fiction."

But fiction is not the opposite of truth. Fiction means "created by imagination." And there is plenty of evidence everywhere in literature and art that imagination can get as close to truth as studious fact-finding can.

This claim is not intended to belittle historians. Most of them do their best to find and state the truth. I like and admire historians, and even associate with some of them. I've had the pleasure of dining, drinking, and conversing with a few of the very best of them, and I've learned a lot from them. Some are even my pen pals, and I cherish their friendship. Why, if I had a daughter who wanted to marry a historian, I wouldn't object on the basis of any innate prejudice against historians. But I might advise her, "Tell him you're the daughter of a historical novelist and see if he still wants to marry you." The fact is, more historians look down on historical novelists than vice versa. And with good reason: There are even more bad historical novelists than bad historians. More on that later.

My hope is that anyone who reads this book, and chances to become a historical novelist, will become one who is respected by good historians.

It can happen. If we study and work conscientiously to raise our image from the old, licentious, stereotypical "bodice-rippers" of our raffish past, we may eventually become comrades-in-arms with the historians who have traditionally scorned us.

Then we can fight proudly alongside them against the common enemy: ignorance of history.

A ROSY PAST

Nostalgia ain't what it used to be.

That statement might sound like a gag, but, actually, it's a smart way to look at the past. I would describe *nostalgia* as "looking at the good old days through rose-colored glasses." But to tell the truth, the good old days *weren't*.

A longing for the good old days is a main motive for writing and reading historical fiction. It's similar to a child's love of fairy tales. Finding it ever harder to anticipate a rosy future, we take refuge in a rosy past: a past when men were chivalrous and brave and honorable, when women were virtuous and neither obese nor anorexic, when our founding fathers were idealistic and selfless, when the happy slaves on the old plantation adored their Massa, when hardy frontiersmen strode into the wilderness to create civilization and enlighten the ignorant savages, when men shouldered their muskets for the one noble purpose of throwing off tyranny and bringing Freedom to all.

And so on.

The trouble with a rosy past, though, is that it doesn't stand up very well under research. Specifically in the case of American history, greed was at least as powerful as idealism: The founding fathers (many of them slaveholders) set up a form of government designed to protect their own advantages; women were chattel; a large percentage of frontiersmen explored new terrains to get beyond the influence of the law, or simply as real estate speculators, like George Washington and Daniel Boone; and many frontiersmen shouldered their muskets because they either yearned to kill "savages" or were afraid of being labeled cowards; they even went to war to defend their right to own slaves.

Clear-eyed research, alas, turns up warts and all.

One of the wonderful ironies of writing about history is that making stuff up doesn't mean it's not true. And obversely, declaring something to be true doesn't guarantee that it is.

—Lucia Robson

True, our nation was the first ever to be created out of whole cloth, right out of the aspirations of enlightened men, and it became the richest and most powerful nation in world history. Americans' inventive genius developed material wealth and creature comforts that the Old World had never imagined. But progress was ruthless, cruel, hypocritical, venal, and relentlessly violent—in other words, no more noble then than now. As one of my favorite essayists, Hal Crowther, puts it, "No one can trump Americans for self-righteous amnesia."

Others agree. "Turning a blind eye to ugly aspects of the past can be a bad habit that carries over into the present," writes columnist Norman Solomon. "Back in 1776, all the flowery oration about freedom did nothing for black slaves, women, indentured servants, or Native Americans. If we forget that fact, we are remembering only fairy tales instead of history."

A good historical novelist has the same obligation as a good historian: to convey a truthful history, not perpetuate pretty myths.

The greatness of America isn't diminished by the recognition that it was made like sausage: the grinding up of human meat—Native American flesh, slave muscle, women's bodies, soldiers' limbs

---

BLURB ME A BLURB

We can't use the word blurb in a historical novel, because it didn't come into use until the early 1900s (after being coined by Gelett Burgess of Purple Cow fame).

Nevertheless, this funny word has assumed an important place in the world of authorship. Writers and publishers want as many blurbs as they can fit on a dust jacket. A blurb is, of course, a "praise phrase" solicited from someone whose opinion counts. It might be as long as a paragraph, or as brief and pungent as a bumper sticker or a Tweet (two other terms we can't use in a historical novel).

You solicit blurbs from people who are likely to praise your work, then you pick out the best parts of the best ones. Literary colleagues are generous with their blurbs, hoping to be praised in their turn. A historical term you *could* use for such mutual admiration is *log-rolling*, an old Congressional phrase meaning, "I'll vote for your bill if you'll vote for mine."

Dick Cady, an old newspaper colleague of mine and a very good writer, sent me the manuscript of his murder mystery and asked if I'd write a blurb for it. I read it and sent back: "This is a pretty blurbworthy book."

He thanked me, then added: "I took the liberty of rephrasing your blurb to express what you really meant to say, which is, 'This is the best mystery novel I ever read.'"

My intent in this book is to encourage you to write historical fiction so authentic and accurate that even real historians will give you a good blurb—maybe even a blurb modified by an adblurb.

(Redcoat, Yankee, and Rebel), laborer sinew, souvenir Filipino fingers .... Telling the truth, even when it's ugly, isn't unpatriotic. Showing the "other side" isn't revisionism; it's a widening of vision.

Therefore, the yearning to tell a great historical narrative isn't an excuse to cherry-pick the glorious parts or ignore the brutality that forms empires.

Much as you the historical novelist might hate to do it, you might have to portray your dashing Virginian protagonist as a male white supremacist, because many such men of the past were. They were brought up that way. Many believed blacks and Indians were inferior, less intelligent races that didn't have souls, an easy excuse to mistreat or kill them with impunity. Between Thanksgiving dinners, those quaint Pilgrims with their white collars and buckled shoes occasionally massacred villages full of Indian women and children, decapitated their chiefs, and displayed their heads on tall poles. Racism was even less subtle then than it is now. Most early American white men thought women should be seen but not heard. As a historical novelist, you might wish to make your hero "politically correct" by today's standards, but if you do that, you'll be lying to your readers.

My wife, Dark Rain, who is also a historical author, spent much of her early life idolizing a brave, beautiful, statuesque female Shawnee Indian chief named Nonhelema. Being of that same tribe, Dark Rain had esteemed her as a heroine. White girls had Clara Barton, Helen Keller, Eleanor Roosevelt, and Amelia Earhart as inspiration; Nonhelema was about the only well-known role model for an Indian girl in Ohio. In the 1990s, my wife got a publisher interested in a novel about Nonhelema and began researching her long, spectacular life story in great detail.

Now and then I would hear my wife mutter in her office, "Oh, no!" Or growl, "You damned fool! How could you?"

"Who's the damned fool?" I asked.

"Nonhelema!" she replied. "This woman did some of the dumbest things! Got involved with no-good palefaces. Believed their promises. Kept doing things for them that were bad for her own people! Drank like a fish! I didn't know this. She's got feet of clay! What kind of a 'heroine' is this, anyway? I'm so disgusted, I'm not sure I even want to write a book about her!"

I sat for a minute with my fingers steepled, amused and musing, then said, "You realize, of course, that your novel keeps
getting better."

She saw my point and didn't like it. "Well, if you like this kind
of a life story so well, you write it!"

"She's your heroine," I reminded her. "It's your book contract."

Eventually she came to terms with it. She asked herself, "So,
Self, you've never made a bad decision? You've never followed
your heart and got into a mess?" She decided to continue writing about the real Nonhelema, warts and all, not the idealized one
she'd admired in childhood naïveté.

As it turned out, we got a better contract for the book from another publisher, and co-authored the novel, adding my knowledge of
the battles and treaties in Nonhelema's life to my wife's understanding
of her culture, spirituality, femininity, and conversion to Christianity.
The book, *Warrior Woman*, was anything but a fairy tale about an ideal heroine. My wife ended up understanding her better than she ever
had—and admiring her more because she persevered through all the
problems she caused herself. As we know, real life is like that.

Even a story about a beautiful woman is better if it includes
warts and all.

FACTUAL AND FICTIONAL FUDGING

One way to compare historians and historical novelists might be
like comparing brunettes and blondes: Novelists have more fun.

Even historians seem to think so. Some admit that they envy us.
It's not just the fun of being free to make up stories. It's also that
we don't have to take ourselves quite as seriously as historians do.
Not *quite*.

To be really good historical novelists, though (and that's what
I want us to be), we have to take our obligation to historical truth

just as seriously as the historians do theirs. But we don't have to bear the burden of being the authority on every factual detail. Our disclaimer is right there on the cover: *a novel.*

My friend and colleague Lucia St. Clair Robson isn't a blonde, but she's one of the good historical novelists, one who makes the work seem like fun. She expresses her attitude about the genre in an almost frolicsome tone: "After all, we really are making stuff up!"

She loves to find factual incidents that add humor and picturesque images to her historical novels, such as an incident in the Second Seminole War when a chieftain named Wild Cat and his warriors attacked a troupe of Shakespearean actors and carried away eighteen trunks full of Elizabethan costumes. The Indians showed up later at treaty talks dressed as Hamlet and his entourage.

It was delightful imagery, but there was a chronological problem: The costume caper occurred after her novel, *Light a Distant Fire*, ended. Says Lucia: "I took a poll among my friends. They all agreed I would be crazy not to use it." So she used it. It was one of only two times she ever "deliberately fudged dates." She explains to me, "I can only plead youth and inexperience as cause for the malfeasance and throw myself on the mercy of the court."

That wasn't even making stuff up. It was simply juggling time to make use of a colorful and amusing scene. In other words, a novelist can have more fun and wiggle room than a historian—although a historian could have put it in parenthetically or as a footnote.

Fun, yes, but notice what Robson said: Only two times did she ever deliberately fudge dates.

The other was when she placed Sam Houston and Davy Crockett simultaneously at the Battle of Horseshoe Bend, when actually they had missed each other by only a short while. That's only two conscious "time cheats" in a long career of novel writing. Many historical novelists take much greater license. Some twist historical chronology in knots to enable late historical figures to encounter each other for dramatic effect. The great novelist E.L. Doctorow felt free to alter just about any historical fact to improve a story, and his works became eminently readable bestsellers. But you certainly wouldn't want to use them as reference books.

Lucia Robson's facts can be trusted if, say, you're a teacher assigning her novels as supplemental reading in a history class. "Researching as meticulously as a historian is not an obligation but a necessity," she tells me. "But I research differently from most historians. I'm looking for details of daily life of the period that might not be important to someone tightly focused on certain events and individuals. Novelists do take conscious liberties by depicting not only what people did but trying to explain *why* they did it."

She adds, "I depend on the academic research of others when gathering material for my books, but I don't think that my novels should be considered on par with the work of accredited historians. I wouldn't recommend that historians cite historical novels as sources."

And they sure don't. They wouldn't risk the scorn of their colleagues by citing novels. But, Lucia adds:

"I think historical fiction and nonfiction work well together. ... I'd bet that historical novels lead more readers to check out nonfiction on the subject rather than the other way around," she says, and then notes:

> One of the wonderful ironies of writing about history is that making stuff up doesn't mean it's not true. And obversely, declaring something to be true doesn't guarantee that it is. In writing about events that happened a century or more ago, no one knows what historical 'truth' is, because no one living today was there.

That's right. *Weren't* there. But *will be*, once a good historical novelist puts us there.

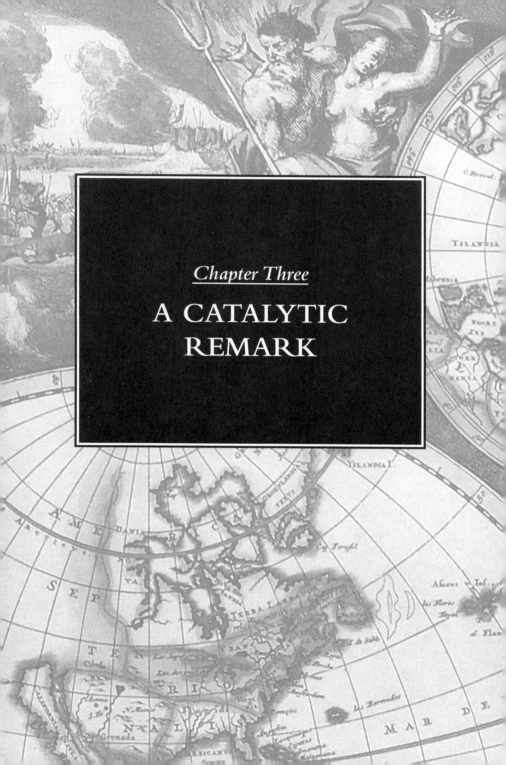

Chapter Three

A CATALYTIC
REMARK

his book probably never would have been written if one of America's most famous historians hadn't said something one day that irked me. His remark was a catalyst.

The late Stephen E. Ambrose was a prodigious researcher and writer, a gruff, big-hearted outdoorsman, a holder of strong opinions that he defended with all the tactfulness of a prickly pear cactus. Due to his powerful personality and the runaway success of *Undaunted Courage*, his biography of explorer Meriwether Lewis, Ambrose was a star spokesman in the national publicity leading up to the Lewis and Clark Bicentennial of 2003–2006. That bicentennial brought us onto the same path or, one might say, into the same channel of the River of Time.

My Shawnee wife, Dark Rain, was a longtime director—one of the three original Native American directors—on the board of the National Bicentennial Planning Council, and I had been writing novels about Lewis and Clark for a quarter of a century, so we often met Stephen on the trail for several years. The last time was at the White House in 2001.

Most historians consider the White House the real starting point of the Lewis and Clark expedition, as that was where President Thomas Jefferson and his secretary, Meriwether Lewis, had developed the purposes and plans for the great voyage of discovery. That's why our delegation of historians, filmmakers, Lewis and Clark descendants, governmental spokesmen, and Western Native American leaders went there that January day—President Bill Clinton's last day in office—for a ceremony in which Clinton posthumously promoted explorer William Clark to the Captain's rank that Jefferson had promised him two centuries earlier.

That day, Stephen was the celebrity historian. He wore a suit and tie to the White House, but it was more common to see him in a misshapen, wide-brimmed hat and a fringed yellow buckskin jacket, part of his camping apparel that he wore when canoeing the Missouri River with his family and other Lewis and Clark aficionados. I dressed up to go to the White House, too, as did most of our delegation. That was the final time I saw Stephen, not long before cancer cut short his travels on the Lewis and Clark Trail that he loved so much.

However, it was a few years earlier that he actually made the irritating remark that started me thinking about the premise of this book. The Bicentennial Council's 1998 annual meeting was in Great Falls, Montana. While my wife was attending meetings, I was working on my novel *Sign-Talker*, about the expedition's Shawnee hunter and interpreter George Drouillard. I took a couple of hours off to hear a panel discussion nearby. Stephen was on the panel with some other trail experts and some Native American tribal elders, and someone in the audience asked a question about an arcane aspect of the expedition. Stephen answered that little was known of it, though it might be an interesting subject for a historical novelist.

"A novelist doesn't have to have facts," he quipped, and the audience laughed. I, who had spent five years in twenty states researching the facts for my Clark family novel *From Sea to Shining Sea*, didn't so much as laugh as snort. *So*, I thought. *One of those historians who looks down his nose at historical novelists and doesn't consider us valid!*

That afternoon, I caught him surrounded by autograph seekers in front of the hotel, and as he signed my copy of *Undaunted Courage*, I thanked him for the remark he'd made about novelists not needing facts. "That tip will save me three or four years on getting out my next novel," I said.

That was about all I had a chance to say on the matter for the rest of the years of our acquaintance. He was a big draw for fundraisers, and with movie negotiations for his Meriwether Lewis book under way, there was seldom a chance to find him without twenty or thirty admirers around.

Now and then we would start to discuss some detail of the expedition on which we didn't see eye to eye, but we never got into a deep conversation before his fans (or, less frequently, one of mine) would squeeze in and crowd around us. So we never got far with any scholarly discussion. I always deferred to him as my elder, not pressing him if he seemed to be getting peevish about a point of contention, even when I knew I was right. It wasn't until that day at the White House that I glanced at a biographical note on him and realized I was three years older than he was. I never got another chance to pull seniority on him.

"A novelist doesn't have to have facts," he quipped, and the audience laughed. I, who had spent five years in twenty states researching the facts for my Clark family novel From Sea to Shining Sea, *didn't so much as laugh as snort.*

But his remark about novelists not needing facts stuck with me, and I began thinking about the relationship between historians and historical novelists, about their relative authority and levels of veracity. Sometimes lecture audiences would ask me questions about the proportions of fact and fiction in my books. And so, eventually, with Stephen Ambrose often in the back of my mind, I began sorting out comparisons and contrasts, and discussed some of my findings during some of my talks at historical societies and writers' workshops.

Some of the chapters in this book have grown out of those considerations. And, not wanting this book to be only Jim Thom expounding on those distinctions, I interviewed several very good, thoughtful historians and historical novelists, whose insights on these matters enrich the discussion that Dr. Ambrose precipitated with a chance remark so many years ago.

And you haven't heard the last of the story about Stephen Ambrose yet, either. This isn't a novel, but it has characters in it, and he's one of the major ones.

COLD CASE

Many of the lessons in this book will refer to the Lewis and Clark expedition and, subsequently, its Bicentennial and the historians, Indians, writers and artists involved in it. That's because it's been such a large part of my own working life for so many years. But the lessons I've learned, and hope to pass on to you, apply not just to American frontier history. If your chosen era is ancient Egypt, or the Bourbon kings, the Mayan empire, the Vikings, the colonization of Australia, or either world war, the researching and storytelling techniques will apply there just as well.

In fact, my first published novel, *Spectator Sport*, was researched like a historical novel, though I began writing it a mere three or four years after the event it covered: the 1973 Indianapolis 500-Mile Race, where I was an eyewitness. It had to be researched well, because the multitudinous facts of the event were on record, and I believed I had an obligation to be accurate.

Most historical research is like what police detectives call a "cold case," where many if not all of the eyewitnesses are gone and most of the evidence has vanished. I had to be especially painstaking in my research for that book because half a million eyewitnesses were still alive, and the details of the event were still fresh in their memories. I didn't want to be caught in errors of fact, even though the plot and the main characters were fictional.

That's usually not a problem with historical fiction. Usually you wish there *were* some eyewitnesses still alive. On the other hand, people who have been dead a century or two don't sue authors who write about them. They might come back and haunt you, but they don't sue.

But here's the key: Whether your historical story is ancient or recent history, what you want to do is re-create it in full—live, colorful, smelly, noisy, savory, painful, repugnant, scary, all the ways it actually was—and then set your reader down smack in the midst of it.

LOOKING FORWARD FROM BACK THEN

Here is the difference between a historian and a historical novelist. This, finally, is my answer to the questions Stephen Ambrose raised in my mind so many years ago.

The historian does this:

He stands before you in the twenty-first century, points back over his shoulder with his thumb, and says, "Two hundred years ago, something happened. Somebody did something that had certain consequences, and now his name and his deed and the time and place are in our history books. Here's what happened...." And then he tells the story of what happened back in the old days.

The historical novelist, though, does this:

He stands beside you, not in the twenty-first century but back in the old days themselves, and says, "Look around! We're at an army camp on the bank of the Missouri in the middle of Indian Country. High Plains. American soldiers have never been up this far before. Hear those drums on the wind? Smell that buffalo roasting over there on the Sioux campfire? My God, man, are you as hungry as I am? As cold? Seems like my feet been wet for a month! Look, here comes Captain Clark down the bluff. Yeah, the big redhead. That Indian with him is Drouillard, our interpreter and the best hunter ever. We'd've starved to death a hundred times if it wasn't for that Drouillard ... Let's go hear what the Cap'n found out from them Sioux. Whether they'll let us proceed up the river, or we have to fight our way past 'em ... Reckon we'll live to see sundown this day, friend?"

And, by then, the readers might be thinking, *Well, if we don't, at least our feet won't be a-hurtin' us anymore! Nor our lousy scalps itchin' no more, neither!*

That's how the historical novelist does it. Not pointing backward toward a past time, but taking the reader back to that time, back when that time was now, and looking forward to the uncertainty of the next hours and days.

The historical novelist has to make that long-ago moment so vivid, so real, so sensuously complete and immediate that the reader is there, then, looking forward, not just here, now, looking back.

That's the *transcendence* I spoke of in the first chapter.

That's Janus, facing backward and forward at once.

FORGETTING THE FUTURE

A novel is supposed to have a plot and suspense.

But how can a historical novelist plot events if he's writing about something that really happened? How can he create suspense when we already know the outcome from our history books? How?

In essence, by immersing the reader so palpably in the past that the history books aren't written yet. That is, by making the reader forget the future.

See what I mean about playing God with time? A historian can't do that, not the way you the historical novelist can.

Don't misunderstand me. I'm not implying that historians can't tell a story vividly and sensuously. Most of the good historians I know are good because they can do that. Stephen Ambrose himself was a master at it. Dayton Duncan, a Lewis and Clark historian, who also wrote scripts for the wonderful documentaries of film-maker Ken Burns, is a master at it. Both of those historians researched the way a good novelist does: by going where the explorers went; by tasting the bison and elk and antelope meat that were so familiar to their subjects; by mustering all the power of imagination to think and feel what the captains and their soldiers thought and felt; by paddling canoes upstream against the relentless current of the Missouri; by standing just where the explorers stood on any specific day of any particular season; and by putting themselves in the moccasins of those men. Good historians can do that as well as a historical novelist can.

But, as historians, they have to point backward from the present and, bearing the authority of their profession, declare what they believe happened back then. Those who read the prose of a historian understand that they're looking *back*.

But we novelists, and our readers, aren't looking back to that time. We are *in* that time, looking forward. We are living in the historical moment, through the vividness of our stories, and looking to the future to find our outcomes.

That requires the good historical novelist to do the same research that a historian does—and then maybe even more.

IT'S FICTION, SO WHY NOT JUST MAKE IT UP?

A novelist could, of course, write a whole novel about any subject or any time without doing any research at all, could just write from imagination, the facts be damned. The resulting novel could be fast-paced, exciting, colorful, intriguing, sexy, and even convey the feeling of a time past. I've read some novels that were done that way, and I've even enjoyed them. Some of those sorts of novels have been researched thoroughly to create authentic landscapes and characters, but the author then has gone on to play fast and loose with real history.

The Flashman series by George MacDonald Fraser were rollicking masterpieces done that way, with notorious gunslingers showing up at the campfires of famous Indian chiefs they actually never met, and so on, just to make fascinating scenes and plot twists. But if they were on any subject that I'd ever studied at all, I could tell those stories were made up, and I wouldn't give them any credibility. Such an author wasn't even pretending to be historically accurate.

If I were a history teacher, I wouldn't assign such yarns as supplemental reading in my classes, because I would want my students to get accurate history, even though they were reading fiction. Another reason why I wouldn't just make up a whole novel is that many regular readers of historical novels are discriminating—if not downright picky—and would dismiss me if they caught me trifling with the historical truth.

Most regular readers of historical fiction are reading to learn, and they gain historical knowledge from story to story. They take pride in having some knowledge they can keep and believe.

An example: Several years after publication of my Clark family novel, *From Sea to Shining Sea*, a novel that began in the Revolutionary War and ended with Lewis and Clark reaching the West Coast, another author wrote a novel with the same title. I saw it in a bookstore. Lo and behold, it, too, was about Lewis and Clark—one of those coincidences that can occur in a world where tens of thousands of books are published every year. I opened it and looked in, just to make sure it wasn't a pirating or a plagiarism of my book, which had become a fairly big seller by then.

Well, it wasn't. The same Lewis and Clark were main characters, and they were going West, sure enough. But while the Shoshone girl Sacagawea was actually the one female member of the Corps of Discovery, there were some other women along on the trail in that author's novel, and they were exotic racial and cultural mixtures. If I remember rightly, one was related to the Czar of Russia or some European royalty. Some elaborate international intrigue had attached them to the expedition, and they were stirring the hormones

GREAT EXAMPLES

One of the best ways to learn how to write good historical novels is to find and read the best ones. Relish them, and try to discern what it is that makes them so good.

I'm often asked, "What's your favorite historical novel?" My reply has evolved over the years. I used to say it was *Northwest Passage*, by Kenneth Roberts. There was a time when I thought it was the best, and I was flattered when someone would compare my *Long Knife* with it.

For a while then, I thought John Barth's *The Sot-Weed Factor* was the best. It was not only a rousing, lusty yarn, sort of a Colonial American "road buddies" adventure, it was full of hilarious wordplay between the protagonists, and showed what rogues many of our first settlers really were.

For dead-on research, sense of time and place, complex but believable characters, and knowledge of maritime life, the British Navy series by the late Patrick O'Brien are unsurpassed. Another great seagoing historical novel is *Ahab's Wife*, by Sena Jeter Naslund, as an example of building fiction upon a fictional character from another novel (*Moby-Dick*).

John Brown, a real-life giant as possessed as Ahab, was finally rendered real and comprehensible to me when Russell Banks portrayed him in *Cloudsplitter*, and there was a while when I would say it might be the best historical novel ever. But often I've reminded myself that *Spartacus*, by Howard Fast, or Tolstoy's *War and Peace* are surely the best.

Now that I'm old enough to make up my mind, I shall let one historical novel fossilize in my opinion as the best ever: It's *Andersonville*, by MacKinlay Kantor. I first read it before I became a historical novelist; now I've reread it after thirty years in the business. If I could have spent those thirty years producing just one historical novel that rich, powerful, and poignant, I'd die happy.

It's your reading assignment. So are all the others I mentioned. And eventually, make your own list.

of the officers and troops something fierce. You could tell that there would be some international diplomatic consequence when the randy young captains got those hot babes to the Pacific coast—maybe the Russian Navy awaiting them, or something. I don't know; I didn't get that far. I suppose I should have read to the end, but on the street outside the bookstore I knew time was running out on my parking meter. So I just put the book back on the shelf and left. Those imaginary hot-blooded heroines had made the novel a matter of no importance to me. The next time I was in that bookstore, a few weeks later, there was no trace of his novel, and the only *From Sea to Shining Sea* the store clerk knew of was mine, and would I mind autographing the ones in stock? Why, happy to, my dear.

My version of *From Sea to Shining Sea* was published in 1984, after five years of painstaking research through twenty states, and more than a year of sweaty-browed labor over the keys of my old

Hermes typewriter. It has sold about half a million copies and is still selling. Many of those copies are used as supplemental reading in American history classes, and some are sold in museums and historical sites wherever those Clarks left their footprints across America— simply because librarians, teachers, even historians, know that the history in the novel is reliable enough.

I'm glad I didn't feel a need to put a nymphomaniacal czarevna in the buffalo robes with the explorers. Inventions like that will ruin you with the historically savvy set. A novelist whose goal is only to tell a rousing tale set in the past is free to juggle facts and dates. There's no law against writing inaccurate historical fiction.

There are many readers who wouldn't care how fanciful it was, so long as they were enjoying it. Some wouldn't know whether it's accurate or not. To them, a costume drama is as good as a reliable historical account. In a playful moment once, I threatened to write a raunchy historical parody called *Lewis and Clark on Brokeback Mountain*. After all, those guys did bunk together for three years.

But I knew better. And in my many years in this business, I've come to respect my readers. Most regular readers of historical fiction are reading to learn, and they gain historical knowledge from story to story. They take pride in having some knowledge they can keep and believe. And so they become more discriminating. They begin to care about the substance of a story, as well as its style. If they see a historian's blurb recommending a historical novel, they might make a mental note and watch for the novelist's next book.

I know this is so, because the readers tell me.

I have no idea how many such serious readers of historical fiction there are, but my publisher used to estimate their number in hundreds of thousands. Two and a half million copies of my historical novels have been sold in the last thirty years, and most readers I meet, or who write to me, say they started with one particular book or another, then made sure they read all the subsequent ones, because, as they tell me: "I just know it must have happened just the way you wrote it," or, "Your stuff checks out with the histories I've read."

Those are the ones I'm most consciously writing for—the ones who want to know the real history, even though they're caught up in the feel of the story. I feel a genuine obligation to give them as much authentic history as I can find and convey.

That is why, Stephen Ambrose, rest your great soul, I, too, need facts.

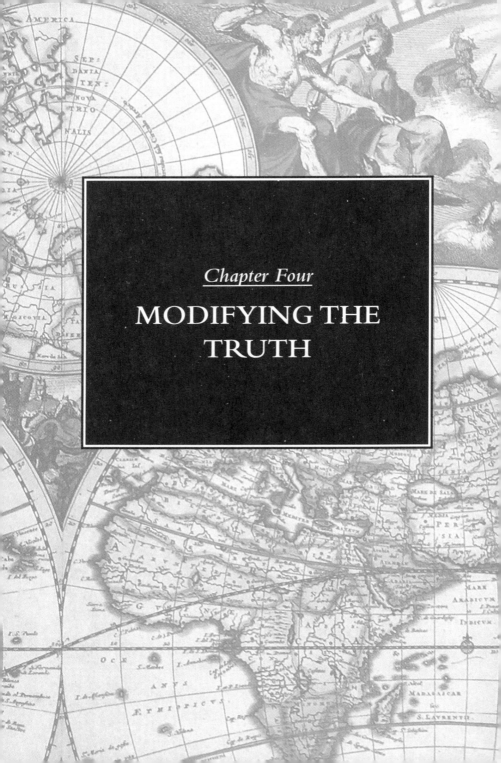

Chapter Four

MODIFYING THE TRUTH

The truth is always being modified. Both a historian and a historical novelist have to know that, in order to know what they're up against. They have to know how elusive truth is. But all the same, they know the truth is the truth, and they must seek it out.

Anyone who intends to tell history has to understand human nature and what human nature does to truth. As we work on books about great historical actions and concepts, we must remember what human perception and memory do to the truth. A good exercise is to look within one's own family.

I had three siblings: an older sister and two younger brothers. Our parents have been dead for many years, but we still get together when we can and entertain ourselves with tales about each other. When we sit around the table doing that, we are being historians. The family history we're telling should be pretty accurate, because we're all eyewitnesses to those things that happened.

However, when I tell about the day my younger brother Bob ran away from home with his stuff tied up in a handkerchief, walked barely beyond sight of the house, and then trudged home three hours later to grumble, "Well, I see you've still got the same old dog," we all have a great laugh about it, except Bob, who denies it ever happened.

One of the many reasons why I wish our mother was still living is that she would look at him and say, "Oh, yes it did, Bob." I have a theory that God gave us parents just to keep us kids from telling family history the way we know it happened. We, in turn, kept our parents' tales truthful.

This is worthy of your attention because this, in a family-sized microcosm, is how history gets made. We remember what we choose to remember, whether we're a family, a town, an ethnic group, a religious sect, a military unit, or a nation.

Another family example is an account given by my friend Sharyn McCrumb, a prize-winning writer of mysteries, historical novels, biographical articles, and short stories. Sharyn is not only an imaginative, vivid, and funny writer, she is also intuitive and wise, in the manner of an Appalachian woman. So, she brings to bear a kind of innate canniness on the details that go into her stories. If something in the record or the spoken account just doesn't seem right, she'll try to analyze what's wrong before she commits it to paper.

She offers "the Burton Beagle story" as a cautionary tale teaching that historical research requires common sense, even when we're listening to a primary source. Here follows, in her own words, an important lesson for any of us who would tell stories that seem true:

> My friend Ward Burton is a race car driver who won the 2002 Daytona 500. He and I have been working on a memoir of his life. Ward told me that when he was six, his father told him that he could have a puppy. Being a huntin' family, specializing in small game, the puppy would of course be a beagle. As Ward tells it, "One Saturday morning my dad took me to a farm where the man had a beagle with a litter of ten pups. We went to the pen and I looked at all those pups and I said, 'Nope. My dog's not here.' And we left."
>
> "You left?" I said.
>
> "Yeah."
>
> "Without a puppy?"
>
> "Yeah."
>
> "And you were six years old?"
>
> "Yeah."
>
> "Then what?"
>
> "The next week he took me to another place with a litter of beagle pups. And I looked 'em all over, and I said again, 'My dog's not here.' And Dad took me home." Ward beamed with

pride at how he had maintained his high standards. "We must'a gone to four or five places before I found the right dog," he says.

"And you were six years old?"

"Yep."

"That doesn't make any damn sense. No six-year-old behaves like that."

"Well, I did."

"Why?" I asked.

"Cause I'm just particular."

A year after I heard that tale, I still thought a big piece of the puzzle was missing, so one day with him in the room, I said to his father, "Tell me about Ward's first dog."

"Well," said his dad, "I was driving down the road one day, and I saw a Beagle puppy by the side of the road with his head stuck in a mayonnaise jar. It was trying to lick the last of the mayonnaise out of the jar, and it got stuck, I reckon. So I stopped to help it. I had to break the jar with a rock, and then I took the pup home and had to file the jar rim off of his neck. So we kept him."

Ward was now muttering, "I forgot about that."

"Did that dog die when Ward was six?" I asked.

"Why, yes," said his dad. "How did you know?"

"Because that's the only thing that makes sense."

"That really impressed Ward. He thought it was magic that I knew there was part of the story missing. But one of my strongest beliefs is that if you have enough information, everything will make sense. If it doesn't make sense, you need to keep digging," Sharyn says. "I use that story when I teach writers' workshops on research. I tell writers that if they come across a true anecdote that doesn't make sense, it means they're missing a key piece of the puzzle, and they have to keep digging."

That's a good lesson to keep in mind throughout any research, whether the eyewitnesses are, like Ward Burton, still alive, or, as in most historical research, long gone down the River of Time. In chapter 12, I'll have Sharyn McCrumb show how that kind of suspicious thinking helped her, while researching historical fiction, to disprove a detail that had been written and repeated by creditable historians. Sometimes fiction writers can modify the truth, and for the better.

Just as my brother put his runaway episode out of memory because it made him laughable, and just as race car driver Ward Burton liked to remember his discrimination in puppy selection, we who deal in history—reading it or writing it—have selective memories. We remember what it suits us to remember. And so, though we want to hear and tell the truth, we modify it. Usually we're not even aware that we're doing so. But sometimes we're doing it deliberately. In most histories, and historical novels, the truth does get modified by human nature.

TEDDY, OUR NATIONAL STORYTELLER

Over the years, the history of a nation just falls together or develops like a photographic print, an overall image made of many random details, of causes and consequences. But sometimes deliberate efforts are made to create an idealized image for the history books. That can complicate research.

The United States of America has been an extremely image-conscious country. At some times more than others, the country's leaders themselves have been like historical novelists, trying to shape the story to match their own conceptions and then sell it to the public like a blockbuster novel.

If any U.S. President ever was a historical novelist at heart, it was Theodore Roosevelt. Having already created his dynamic image of himself, he instituted studies and wrote yarns and histories designed to make the world see America the way he wanted it to be seen.

American history was to Roosevelt the "magnificent westering," that inevitable advance of white Anglo-Saxon Protestant civilization into the savage West, sometimes called "Manifest Destiny." Roosevelt encouraged historians and archaeologists to help interpret and write the narrative of America to suit him.

I tell writers that if they come across a true anecdote that doesn't make sense, it means they're missing a key piece of the puzzle, and they have to keep digging.

—Sharyn McCrumb

Part of that narrative required a way of whitewashing the destruction of the Native American cultures whose land this had been for tens of millennia. Civilization of America had to be presented as a predestined step up from primitive existence. It had to seem *good* that the Indians would vanish. Archaeologists were empowered to take over their bones and artifacts, and historians were encouraged to take the Indians' history away from them and restate the story as the natural dominance of intrepid white heroes over a backward race that would have vanished anyway.

It was easy to take away the Indians' history; they didn't have their own history books that would have had to be burned (and, as some inadvertent humorist once said, "Oral history isn't worth the paper it's written on"). It was the "survival of the fittest," cowboy and Indian style: cowboys superior. We would call it Social Darwinism now. Hollywood picked up on it, and we grew up believing Teddy Roosevelt's version of the inevitable "improvement."

Like most Americans my age, growing to adulthood without
ever seeing a TV set, I'd gotten my image of American history
from the standard history texts, from magazines and newspapers
and comic books, from radio and from movies. I also spent much
of my time in my hometown's Carnegie Library, checking out
countless books, both nonfiction and fiction.

In school, I read the so-called American classics of Washington Irving, Herman Melville, and James Fenimore Cooper. I de-
voured young people's novels about noble, clean-living young
frontiersmen and Indian fighters, like Joseph Altsheler's intrepid
Henry Ware, who might be described as a teenage Davy Crockett
without the character flaws. The movies I went to displayed John
Ford's vast western scenery and those hard-bitten but noble heroes
played by John Wayne and Glenn Ford, Henry Fonda, Randolph
Scott, and so on. All square-jawed, brave, upstanding and *white* pioneers taming the Wild West. That is, Teddy Roosevelt's version
of America's noble and inevitable growth.

Fortunately for me, Mark Twain grew to be my favorite American author, planting a seed of wry skepticism, but that didn't
sprout until later.

FIRST IMPRESSION

In the 1970s, when the time came for me to write my first historical
novel, I had learned what a conquering hero in Teddy Roosevelt's
American saga was supposed to look and act like. The hero I chose
gave the impression of being perfect for the role. He was, in fact,
one of Teddy Roosevelt's personal heroic favorites.

Maybe I shouldn't say the one I chose, but the one who chose
me. I hadn't intended to write historical novels. But the United
States Bicentennial was coming up, I was an Indiana native, and
the only notable Revolutionary War hero Indiana could claim was

the handsome, athletic, courageous, and visionary young Virginia militia leader George Rogers Clark, who had come out here in 1778 with a ragged little band of frontier militiamen and seized this whole territory from the British—arguably the most amazing and significant victory in that whole war. There wasn't yet a place called Indiana back then, but part of that territory would eventually become my native state. As the bicentennial activities loomed and programs developed, somebody from the Indiana Historical Society got in touch with me and suggested that I should write some sort of a drama, a novel, a play, an outdoor pageant, or even an opera about Clark, to coincide with the two hundredth anniversary of his achievement.

Remembering Clark from my boyhood readings, I knew it was a most stirring story. I began researching Clark, and I got a New York publisher fired up about a historical novel that I could complete in time for publication at the appropriate moment. I suggested the title *Long Knife*, the name the Indians gave Clark, and I threw myself into the task of bringing him to life.

I soon realized that few modern Americans even knew who Clark was. Hearing the name, they presumed that I meant the Clark of Lewis and Clark (who was his youngest brother). Historical knowledge fades fast. I saw that book as a chance to re-educate American readers about the young hero who gave them much of the Midwest, and this gave me more impetus to complete the novel.

As a historical researcher, I was a total novice, but the more I learned of Clark, the more motivated I became. For the first time as a struggling novelist, I was writing about someone who inspired me. I wanted readers to admire that young patriot as much as I did, and to appreciate his daring, his innate leadership qualities, and the physical and moral toughness that helped him lead a band of rustic riflemen through one of the hardest physical ordeals in

IS MY STORY OLD ENOUGH?

History never ends. Its consequences are always with us, influencing our present and our future. It doesn't have a beginning, either. Whatever we decide its beginning was, something preceded that. When you have a story in mind, you might ask yourself whether it's old enough to be historical.

Among those of us who write of historical events, there's a joke: "The last eyewitness is dead at last! Now we can tell it the way we know it was."

Sounds like something right out of a criminal court case, doesn't it? There are similarities. The simple fact is that the history of any event begins the moment it happens. Today's newspaper story or TV news script is the beginning of a written historical account that will either vanish or evolve into history books. And those history books will keep being revised forever, as long as anyone's interested.

Witnesses—veterans and victims—of World War II, Korea, and Vietnam still live, but histories have been and are being written. Histories of the wars in Iraq and Afghanistan are already being published even as the fighting continues. So, obviously, there's no age minimum for a history.

And not all histories are of war. Social movements and economic and environmental developments evolve forever. It's just harder to establish their durations, as they aren't marked by formal declarations, truces, or peace treaties.

So it's enigmatic. You'll decide you're writing a historical novel if it seems "past" to you—even though we know history flows on and there has been no real finality, no real past. It's history if you say so.

Just pretend you're God with a stopwatch.

military history. I sensed that readers wouldn't fully appreciate the feat unless I could, through the evocative power of this great English language of ours, make them see, hear, taste, smell, and feel the whole narrative as if they were right there in the midst of it with him: the horrendous cold, hunger, pain, fatigue, and doubt that eventually led to such a triumph.

Though I was a newcomer to the genre, I'd had some good preparations for making that kind of a tale: I had, as I mentioned in the first chapter of this book, a keen sense of being immersed in the flow of history. I had generations of soldiering American ancestors, beginning in that same Revolutionary War. I had wintered in Korea as a Marine, so I knew fatigue, cold, pain, and fear quite well. I'd had all that heroic reading, of the Teddy Roosevelt sort, so I knew what to admire in men who wrested America from the savage, primitive wilderness.

And, I'd had a teacher of creative writing—Dr. Werner Beyer of the Butler University English Department—who had given me the best four-word piece of advice I ever got: *Write to their senses!* I had taken that to heart.

Another piece of good timing was that a Butler University history professor, Dr. George Waller, was working on a volume called *The American Revolution in the West*. A few discussions with him helped me get the big picture of what Clark's achievements really meant for the new republic.

Another advantage I had was that I knew the territory. I had run the woods as a boy right here where Clark did his great deeds, so I had a feel for the landscape, the climate. I knew and could describe the woods and prairies and the specific plant species that he and his men had passed through. They traveled by horse and canoe back then, and I knew horses and canoeing. Everything you have learned in life can count as research material, if it's relevant to the story you're going to tell.

Of course, imagination would be one of my most powerful tools in the telling of Clark's story. I intended to show the narrative through his own eyes, so I had to imagine myself right into the heart and mind and soul of Clark. I had to imagine how he felt about what he was doing; I had to imagine his motives and his doubts; I had to imagine how he felt about God and about his family and about his duty to his homeland of Virginia—all the traits that existed in a man I'd never met, I needed to imagine, and imagine powerfully enough that I could make myself, and my reader, walk in Clark's shoes through that great risk and triumph of his. That would require every bit of my imaginative power.

Imagination, yes. But even in my first historical novel I wanted as much truth as I could ascertain. I don't remember just how I determined to be that conscientious about historical accuracy so many years ago, but I probably thought that the whole Indiana Historical Society would be looking over my shoulder as I told that story. I guessed its members knew more facts about Clark than I knew. In fact, some volunteered to share their expertise and resources with me when they learned that I was undertaking the job. I was a novelist, getting myself stirred up to write in a white heat of creativity one of the most exciting stories that had ever happened in these parts. But there was something keeping me in check. It was the sense that I had a responsibility to history itself. I would have to do intense research, probably in dusty libraries and museums—not a creative writer's favorite pastime. But I wanted to write the truth, as closely as any two hundred-year-old truth could be found, and beyond that, I wanted verisimilitude.

VERISIMILITUDE?

That is one of the most important words in the historical fiction business: verisimilitude.

You might want to print it out in bold Magic Marker and put it on the wall right above your desk where you'll see it every time you look up from the keyboard: *VERISIMILITUDE: The appearance or semblance of truth.* As Mark Twain once said, the difference between history and fiction is that fiction has to be believable.

To put it as Sharyn McCrumb might, a six-year-old boy turning down one cute puppy after another because he's "particular" doesn't have verisimilitude. But a boy missing his puppy that had died, looking for that exact missing puppy in litter after litter and not seeing it yet, that does have verisimilitude.

The same way that a young Ward had the familiar puppy image in his mind because of the one he'd known, I had an image of the ideal young frontier hero I was going to write about, and I had that image because I'd grown up in a culture colored by Teddy Roosevelt's imagination. Like my wife and her desire to make the Shawnee woman chief like the one she had imagined in girlhood, I wanted George Rogers Clark to be admirable in every way according to the American myth. I wanted him to make a stunning impression on his return to the pantheon of American heroes. I wanted all his motives to be seen as noble. And so, when I researched his life, I eagerly seized the things that made sense in such a hero.

For instance, in researching his education, I was pleased to find that among the authors he'd read in his student days were Euclid and Marcus Aurelius. Euclid made sense, as Clark became a surveyor as a young man, and Euclid's mathematics are the foundation of surveying. As for Aurelius, the calm, bold, grave words in his *Meditations* were in perfect tune with the calm, bold, grave demeanor that Clark exhibited whenever the going really got tough:

> There is a proper dignity and proportion to be observed in the performance of every act of life.
>
> Perform every act in life as if it were your last.

Nothing happens to anybody which he is not fitted by nature
to bear.

It made sense. A youth who had memorized such precepts would be
a man who lived and acted as Clark did. There was verisimilitude.

I searched everywhere I could think of for clues to the soul
and manner of the remarkable young man I was going to portray.
I researched his genealogy and the colonial Virginian agricultural society in which he'd grown up, and their religious beliefs,
and their neighbors (including Thomas Jefferson), and the political developments of that time when the colonials were turning
against King George. I studied their pastimes, their sports, their
joy in the hunt, their social customs, their class-conscious marriage matches, and their love of, and greed for, land.

*I was a novelist, getting myself stirred up to write in a
white heat of creativity one of the most exciting stories that
had ever happened in these parts. But there was something
keeping me in check. It was the sense that I had a responsibility to history itself.*

In that study, I came to feel something they felt then but we
don't now: the awareness that beyond the mountains, populated
only by pesky savages, lay the richest and most fertile lands imaginable, already granted by the kings of England to Virginia—
land, that is, to which Virginians felt entitled. This was an agricultural society in those days, before the Industrial Revolution.
Land was the wealth of such a people, and it was there for the
taking. All that stood in the way were the restraints imposed
by King George III of England, and a few thousand disorga-
nized Indians.

Imagine the excitement of knowing there was a frontier, that your God had destined you to cross it, and that it was yours for the taking if you could get there first!

I was able to imagine that feeling because Teddy Roosevelt had set me up for it.

I gave Teddy himself no conscious thought while I was forming that book in my mind, but he had prepared me to imagine both that tempting wilderness and the heart and mind of George Rogers Clark, a man totally unlike my real, modern self. That made it possible for me to admire him enough that I was willing to spend years researching him, getting inside his skin, and writing his saga so vividly that readers understood him and felt they were with him during those terrible sufferings and the amazing final triumph.

Research did show that the young frontier superman wasn't flawless, of course. He often had to subdue a temper signaled by his red hair, and he certainly knew what the bottom of a whiskey or rum bottle looked like. He was accused of being more ruthless than we'd like our heroes to be, but that allegation was usually based on what his enemies said about him, when they had to explain how he had bested them. Political enemies slandered him, and creditors dogged him throughout his postwar life. He might have preferred to die a young man at his moment of triumph.

By the time I'd finished my research, I had still another focus for my admiration of Clark: He was a military leader who didn't squander lives. He used bluffing and an understanding of his foe's psychological weaknesses and fears to win objectives with a minimum of bloodshed. His topsy-turvy victory at the siege of Vincennes, which took out of British control all the land between the Great Lakes and the Ohio River, was achieved without a single one of his soldiers being killed.

As I said in the beginning of this book, though, few great stories have happy endings. Forsaken by his state of Virginia after the Revolution, Clark died a besotted, poverty-stricken, bitter, one-legged old bachelor, who might have recognized his destiny in one of Marcus Aurelius's own lines:

> As for life, it is a battle and a sojourning in a strange land; but the fame that comes after is oblivion.

George Rogers Clark's story was thus the first lump of clay I ever grabbed up from the past to shape into a historical novel. My book about him has been on the shelves for a long time, and I've heard from hundreds of readers that they were deeply moved and inspired by it.

Just yesterday I got letter from a career soldier in the U.S. Army, who said he carried *Long Knife* everywhere his duty took him, in warfare and peace, referring to George Rogers Clark as an exemplary officer, whom he always emulated. He said he wore out five paperback copies.

The most important person in my life, though, hasn't read it and doesn't intend to: my wife, whose Shawnee people were devastated more by Clark than by any other man in history. He repeatedly led autumn expeditions into Ohio to burn their villages and crops and leave them starving and homeless through the winters.

I tell her, "But even the Shawnee warriors and chiefs he fought admired him as a great enemy. If there was a treaty, Clark was the only white man they wanted to talk to. If you read *Long Knife,* you'll at least see what they admired in him."

Gently she replies, "You don't get it. I don't *want* to admire him."

Actually, I do get it. Teddy Roosevelt's modification of the historical truth isn't all that palatable to American Indians.

RETROSPECTION:
LESSONS LEARNED

Thirty-seven years have passed since the publication of *Long Knife*. It is still in print after three different editions. Its hero, George Rogers Clark, has appeared in three or four of my subsequent novels, and I've written nonfiction articles about him for historical periodicals and anthologies, so he is always fresh in my mind, and I keep learning more about him. He is still just as amazing to me as he was while I was first portraying him as a revolutionary hero.

But because of research for subsequent books about his time and place in history, I've discovered some modifications I might make if I were just now writing that first book about him. The two main changes I might make would be about context.

First, I would revise some of the scenes in which he was intimidating or winning over the Indians. I didn't know then, but know now, how Indians really would have assessed the words and manner of such a man. I had never known Indians when I wrote that book, so their reactions to him I could interpret only through his own writings, or through the perceptions given by historians who had studied his accounts, that is, the archival research sources. Now I've spent twenty-five years deeply involved with Indians of many different tribes.

Of course, the chieftains and warriors he dealt with would have been impressed by his bold talk and his seeming fearlessness; I'm sure I had that right. What I didn't know then was that the Indians had other, more pragmatic, reasons to go along with him, reasons other than just his challenging words. I hadn't known enough about the Indians themselves to realize that they weren't naïve about him. They had a sophisticated understanding about the dangers his arrival in the West created for their villages. They knew that their practical alliance with the British might have to change, because the close presence of his American militiamen could harm the tribes more than the distant British could help them.

Those tribal leaders also had friendships and trading ties with the French settlers there in the Mississippi Valley, and those Frenchmen would have advised the Indian leaders that they should open their ears to the American newcomer. Clark had brought with him the news that France and the Americans had signed a treaty of alliance against the British. Always caught in the middle when white men's forces fought over their territory, the chiefs had to pay keen attention to the way the winds of advantage blew.

When Clark later wrote his report of a chief brashly ripping the English flag off his breast and declaring his allegiance to "the Long Knife," Clark reasonably assumed that his own oratory alone had swayed the chief. But the chief likely had made up his mind already, after counsel with the Frenchmen and other chiefs and a careful assessment of his own best interests. His symbolic casting off of the British colors would have been a typical Native American dramatic flourish, which Clark naturally saw as evidence of his own powers of persuasion.

Historians have taken Clark's assumption at face value, and have read it the way he wrote it. I, as a new historical novelist, gave credence to his perception, and theirs, and wrote it that way in the novel. It wasn't until later, after deeper research, and years among Indians, that I understood how I might have oversimplified those dramatic moments. Since I was writing the story through Clark's point of view, it was, of course, appropriate to write it as he'd seen it. But I could have given a more nuanced history lesson if I'd known more about the context, and hinted at the other factors that swayed the chiefs to Clark's side.

The other, and larger, context of George Rogers Clark's story was that the expansion of America was always a narrative of land speculation. Before the Revolutionary War, young Clark was, as I said, a surveyor, working for the wealthy Virginians who had their eye on the rich lands beyond the Allegheny Mountains. When Clark went to Williamsburg to get their support for his foray into the distant Mississippi Valley, he knew, and they understood, too, that if he succeeded, he would not only protect Virginia's vulnerable outback from the British and their Indian allies; he would also seize control of that fertile watershed and the rivers that could carry its products to the seas. Those famous and powerful Virginians, Thomas Jefferson, Patrick Henry and George Wythe, were thinking expansion as much as security. They believed the western country was rightfully Virginia's by charter, and so they schemed to gain support for his daring plan.

If I were to modify my George Rogers Clark novel now, I might spend a few more paragraphs emphasizing how his preemptive strike against the British in the west was motivated also by Virginia's land lust. I vaguely understood that when I wrote the book. But my portrayal of young Clark as "Virginia's westward blade" in the War for Independence was more appealing than, say, "George Rogers Clark, real estate speculator" would have been.

The slowly learned lesson is this: You must resist the propensity to see history only as you want to see it. You must look for reality beyond what you were raised to believe.

In short, your head will lead you to research deeper than your heart will.

THE RELENTLESS FLOW

All this personal, political, and geographical musing I've just done here on George Rogers Clark is to show that if you would be a historical novelist, you must know much more than you write. Your characters do what they do in the context of real history. No matter how important their deeds and their personalities are, they are swept along in the current of the great historical stream.

Your characters are who they are because they enter that stream when and where they do. They are products of their time, and they do what they do because of the circumstances of history in which they find themselves. They may influence the course of that stream, the way a dam or a logjam or a deluge of rain may influence the course of a river, but they are still carried along in the stream, which has been flowing forever.

This is the big truth that the historical novelist must never forget. History moves on with a force, and we who participate in it can always feel the force. The clock on your office wall and the appointment calendar on your desk, the hunger you feel several times a day, even the urgings of your bowels and bladder and the arthritis in your knees are palpable reminders of the moving force of time. And, if the characters in your historical novel are going to have any verisimilitude, they, too, must feel the force of time, and your reader must feel them feeling it. You the writer want to move the whole reader, not just his eyeballs.

It is that forceful, palpable flow of time that makes the "truth" of a narrative so hard to fix. Truth is distorted and blurred by the turbulent flow of time around it. Our wisdom grows with age, or we regress. Our perceptions change. New information appears, some good, some bogus. Mores and ethics change. Public opinions evolve. Tolerance expands or shrinks.

All those influences cause us to modify our perceptions of historical truth as time flows on. Is it any wonder that history is forever in revision?

We who write of history, whether historians or novelists, must keep that revision going.

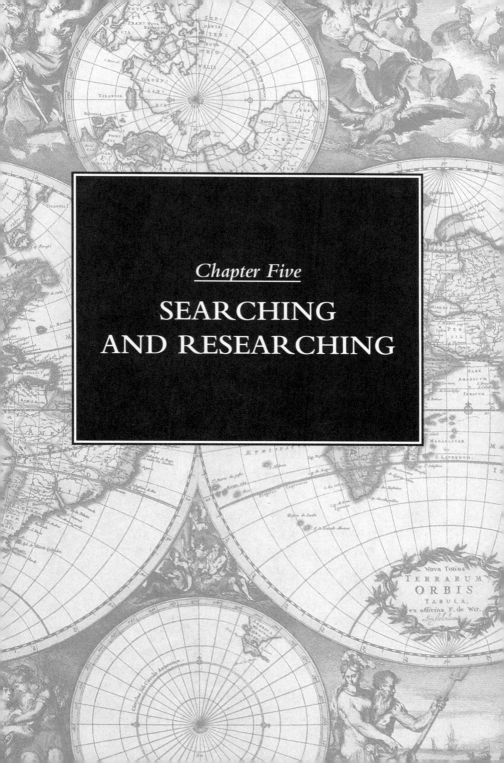

Chapter Five

SEARCHING
AND RESEARCHING

hen I teach at writers' conferences, or just chat with readers, two of the most frequent questions are "Where do you get your ideas for those stories?" and "How do you research all that old stuff?"

The answers are connected.

Several of the ideas that eventually became my novels have been in my mind since childhood, because I grew up immersed in history. But some of the best ideas first turned up when I was researching earlier novels, and grew in my mind until I had to develop them into separate novels.

The answer to the second question is, "I research any way I can think of."

It came as a pleasant surprise to me, when I got busy in the historical genre, that doing research is at least as exciting and fascinating as doing the writing. Sometimes the giant task of finding all the facts you need to know turns into a life adventure. Research, if you do it right and if you enjoy learning, can be so engrossing that you'll be reluctant to quit it and sit down to do the actual writing.

As I said, you have to know much more than you write. Regardless of Stephen Ambrose's facetious remark, a good historical novelist does have to have facts. And more facts. And more and more facts.

After a long career of going after those facts, of "finding all that old stuff," I can give some pretty good advice on how to do it. Ask me ten years from now, and I'll be able to give even better advice, because I keep learning all the time.

STANDING ON THE SHOULDERS OF OTHERS

To begin, you should know that you'll depend on the work and experience of many, many other people. The word research obviously means "to search again." You'll be searching for facts, knowledge, and understandings already gained and held by persons before you. Historians and historical novelists alike stand on the shoulders of their predecessors. You will sort through, select, and recycle what they have already learned.

A writer named Wilson Mizner once said, "If you steal from one author, it's plagiarism; if you steal from many, it's research." That has become a classic aphorism among historians and historical novelists, usually quoted with a sheepish grin.

Not all the knowledge you'll use is written knowledge. Though archives are a main source, there are other sources, such as oral histories and old pictures, artifacts in museums, and your own memory of historical facts that you've been taught.

But even those unwritten sources come to you through the efforts of others. However successful you may become as a historical novelist, keep yourself humble by remembering the debt you owe to the work of others.

CREATIVE RESEARCH

Creative writing. That's what a novelist does. But if you're a historical novelist, you must also do creative research.

Although research is, as I just stated, built upon the original work of others, it can and must be done creatively. I, as a veteran researcher, might list research sources and methods for you to follow, but you yourself must innovate—be creative—as you put together the facts and understandings you need for your novel. That's why I'm not going to list the research sources that I frequently use. Another reason is that there are simply too many of them. To list even a fraction of the ones I know would fill this book, and I know only a fraction of those that exist and are useful. You're welcome to stand on my shoulders, but you'd better stand on many others' shoulders, too.

Living is a creative process, because only you can conduct your own unique life. Likewise, only you can conduct the research for your own unique story. Only you, the author, will able to pose your own questions, because only you will have a sense of where your story is going and what facts you need to get it there.

....

Not all the knowledge you'll use is written knowledge. Though archives are a main source, there are other sources, such as oral histories and old pictures, artifacts in museums, and your own memory of historical facts that you've been taught.

....

The very popular and prolific late novelist James Michener was, at times and in a broad sense, a historical novelist, though he's not usually categorized that way. When he wrote about Hawaii, Chesapeake Bay, the American West, or the lands of the Bible, he spanned the distant past—often going even as far back as their origins in geological time, moving forward through the development of their aboriginal peoples and through their successive civilizations—into the present. Michener did so much historical research for his giant novels that eventually he hired researchers to help mine the archives and amass the factual data he needed. If you're successful enough, you can afford to do that. It was just one of the kinds of creative research methods he developed.

If you can't afford to hire a research staff, but happen to have friends who are traveling or working in the right places, you can ask them to look things up for you. Peter Guardino, an Indiana University historian who spends much time researching in Mexico for his own Mexican-American War history book, was helpful to me when I wrote a novel about that conflict. British historian John

Sugden has answered questions for me from his home in England. Even if you don't have friends who can help, you can do some research on the experts in your area of interest and politely query them if you need help verifying specific information.

If you're lucky enough to be married to someone who knows how to research, or if you have scholarly offspring, research can become a family enterprise. I'm fortunate to be married to a woman who is a natural researcher: diligent, curious, resourceful, and with research interests that are parallel to mine. As I mentioned in an earlier chapter, we have even co-authored a novel, and she has written a section in this book on genealogical research, one of her strengths.

I have even been offered research help by total strangers, persons who have read my books and say they'd love to be involved in digging out anything I might need. That is flattering, but I've seldom taken anyone up on it. And the reason for this is the same as why I wouldn't depend on a research team, even if I could afford one: I wouldn't rely solely on a volunteer I'd sent scouting into the archives, beyond some specific fact. Someone sent to find a specific bit of historical data tends to look single-mindedly for that particular thing, resulting in a kind of tunnel vision. I'd rather do it myself, because many of the best things I've ever found first appeared "in the corner of my eye," so to speak—things that likely would have been ignored by someone sent to look for a particular fact. The best and most consequential example occurred in 1978 while I was researching the life of George Rogers Clark for *Long Knife*. Using an old book to trace that period of his youth when he was surveying wilderness land in the Kanawha River Valley before the Revolutionary War, I just barely noticed the fact that a white woman had passed through that rugged valley nearly twenty years earlier, crossing the Allegheny Mountains in making her escape from Shawnee Indians who had kidnapped her during the French and Indian War. I was too busy pursuing Clark's career to get sidetracked into that little story, but it intrigued me enough that I went back to my notes after the Clark book was finished and began checking out that obscure incident. It then formed the basis for my second historical novel, *Follow the River*, which has been in print since 1981 and has sold one and a half million copies.

If I'd sent a hired researcher to look for that part of my Clark story, I never would have caught that peripheral glimpse of an unrelated story which eventually was to become the basis for the most successful of all my books.

GREAT LIBRARIES

The information we historians and historical novelists need has always been at our fingertips. But our fingertips weren't always tapping at a computer keyboard in order to bring it up on a screen of pixels. No, back then our fingers walked through the alphabetical card files of libraries—those deep trays of three-by-five-inch file cards on which were printed all the details we needed to find books, periodicals, and collections in the library. We'd write notes on what we needed, and librarians would go fetch the material for us, or we'd go into the stacks ourselves and find the books and folders. We could find just about anything we needed with the index-card system, just as well as Internet users can today. The big difference was that we had to leave home to do it.

Much of what I've needed in my long writing career exists in a magnificent library only fifteen miles from where I live: the Indiana University Library in Bloomington. The stacks seem endless. The place is well-lit and provides desks and chairs where the researcher can sit with a pile of books, some so old they're bound in real leather, and browse and take notes in studious silence—no Muzak!—as late as midnight during the school terms. It's comfortable as home, being climate-controlled for the preservation of the valuable old documents. The sense of intellectual concentration prevails. I remember looking up from a stack of materials about the Northwest Ordinance one night and seeing a female student at a nearby desk so absorbed in her own heap of books that she had started drooling. She wiped her mouth on her sleeve, saw me watching, and blushed. Reflexively, I wiped my own mouth, because for all I knew, I might have been drooling too, in my own studious trance.

Considerably farther from home was the American historical researcher's mother lode: the Library of Congress in Washington, DC. Any time I started research on a novel, I went there first, and it was like a pilgrimage to the heart of my country. I checked in at a modest hotel for as many days as I thought I'd need, then went to the great library. That main reading room is an inspiring surround of architectural splendor, bustling with scores of helpful staffers who wheel to your desk cartloads of requested books, and even guide you to related materials. If you want to feel like a valued citizen of your country, that's the place to visit. When my brief-case finally was crammed with all the notes and copies I thought I needed, including information on where in America to look for special collections, I would make my other routine stops to visit with friends and colleagues.

As my last stop of the pilgrimage I'd go to the Lincoln Memo-rial, where I'd gaze up at that statue of the greatest writer who was ever President of the United States. I'd give him silent greetings from southern Indiana, where we both grew up. Then, inspired by the big-hearted prose of his second Inaugural Address, I'd leave that city and head out to whatever other capitals, libraries, battle-fields, museums, and historical societies I'd need to visit on the way home to my old clackity typewriter and the self-imposed solitary confinement I needed to start writing the novel.

You who can sit at your computer in your own room and fetch all that kind of data with your fingertips have that advantage, but you may be missing something supremely important. If your research doesn't lead you physically through the historic countryside where your stories actually took place, you may miss much of the needed inspiration for your intended work. Sitting before a screen at home, maybe just in your underpants, might be wonderfully quick and efficient. But doing historical research is like savoring hickory nuts or making maple sugar: What makes it really good is getting right into the middle of it.

Sense of place is very important, and you can't experience that by just sitting at your computer. Get off your keyboard and do some research that requires you to experience history physically.

THE BIBLIOGRAPHY: A RUNNING START IN A SITTING POSITION

Historians advertise their credibility by listing their sources. The bibliography section of a history book is testimony to the wry maxim that research is stealing from many authors. Actually, historians borrow, not steal, from each other. They guide each other and give attribution to each other's work. Later in this book, I'll let some of those historians tell you how they do that, and what they feel about it. It's important for historical novelists to know what historians are doing.

A thorough bibliography is an impressive testimony to the historian's conscientious and industrious search for the truth of the matter. (You will seldom, by the way, see a historian list Google or random Web sites in the bibliography; I'm pretty sure of that.) The bibliographies and indexes in history books are your best and quickest guides to where all that old information can be found. You can sit in your chair and get a running start before you ever check a book out of a library.

Of course, you'll read the rest of the history book itself, if it's directly related to your topic, to give yourself background and insights. The aspects of the history that will be most pertinent to your novel can be found alphabetically arranged in the index.

Indexes and bibliographies of other primary sources can be immensely helpful in your own research. You should read as many as you can of the sources cited in the bibliography, then go through the bibliographies in those books in their turn. Your head and your notebooks will begin to fill up with relevant historical facts. In many history books, you'll also find maps, old illustrations, and vivid descriptive prose. Those are very important, too, because when you start writing, you'll need to convey not just facts but rich, detailed visual images.

NOVELS AS SOURCES

If historians can borrow from each other, and historical novelists can borrow from historians, can historical novelists borrow from other novelists? Well, they'd be fools not to. A historical novelist researching the gold rush would certainly not pass up the power and vividness of Jack London's novels and stories, because London had participated in those harrowing ventures and described just how they looked and felt. If you want to write a historical novel about the English class system, what better background than the novels of Fielding, Dickens, and Brontë? As for old Europe, say, post-Moorish Spain, one of the earliest novels is the best: *Don Quixote*. When Cervantes wrote that masterpiece, he wasn't writing a "historical" novel per se, but his tragicomic protagonist was living so deeply in the chivalric past that he was gloriously delusional and pathetically anachronistic. There was a novelist who really knew how to play God with time!

Yes, indeed, some of the richest veins of meaning, imagery, and truth may be mined just by reading fiction for pleasure. Anything that supplies facts, expands your mind, and enriches your soul will likely make you a better novelist in your own time, and that qualifies it as research.

You'll hardly ever find novels listed in any historian's bibliography. But some historians have admitted that they became historians after being originally enchanted through good novels. And good writers are often good readers, first.

If you do a good enough job as a historical novelist now, you might even help create a future historian or two. Or you might do so by writing such a lousy historical novel that it'll inspire some soul to become a historian, just to set history right. But it's better to try to be a good example than a bad one.

HANDS ON THE PRIMARY SOURCES

Whether you're a Web browser or a bookworm, you'll begin to find references to primary source documents, old manuscripts, diaries, memoirs, and collections. Those can be wonderful references, helping to bring moments to life. Often they contain mundane descriptions of daily life, of land and money transactions, lawsuits, wills, and countless details that the historian chose not to use but a historical novelist might. A nice touch in a historical novel is, say, a scene in which the novel's hero or heroine sits with a quill pen writing a letter or a diary page that actually still exists in an archive somewhere. You, the author of the novel, can describe the piece of paper or parchment or the diary page on which it's being written, and at the same time use the actual words composed by the person who wrote it so long ago. The emotional impact of such a device can be strong.

For example, I remember finding in the document section of the Filson Club, a historical society in Louisville, Kentucky, the actual death certificate that George Rogers Clark had to write after the loss his dear friend and second-in-command, Joseph Bowman. Major Bowman died from inhaling the smoke and fire of an accidental gunpowder explosion. The irony was heart-wrenching: Bowman was supervising the firing of cannons in celebration after their capture of the British fort at Vincennes, that amazing conquest in which, as I mentioned earlier, not one of Clark's soldiers died in combat. Sparks set off an accidental explosion in the powder stores, and Bowman died of scorched lungs a few days later, victim not of a battle but a victory celebration. By the time I wrote that scene, both Clark and Bowman were so much a part of me that the image of Clark writing his friend's death certificate was heart-breaking. As I held that certificate in my hand two centuries later—the certificate itself, not a copy of it—his penning of it was not just an image in my imagination, it was a personal experience. Such evocative moments occur during the adventure of deep research. You won't find them while browsing the Internet.

THE DANGER OF IMMEDIACY

When using old documents, keep in mind that there are advantages and disadvantages, both of which can affect the point of view from which your story is being told. One advantage, of course, is that those things were written in "real time"—that is, when the events were actually happening, or immediately afterward. So there is a fresh immediacy about them. They might even have been written by eyewitnesses or by persons hearing directly from eyewitnesses or by family members moved by the events. They are as close as you can come to interviewing someone who was involved in or affected by the incidents. To them, this wasn't a "cold case." It was happening NOW.

That same immediacy, though, can be a disadvantage for a writer seeking the truth. Remember, persons involved in events are not usually objective witnesses. They tend to write their accounts according to the way they feel about them. If they were principal actors in the event, they might "spin" the account so as to take all possible credit or avoid blame. If the event involved an enemy or a rival, the account might be written to preempt, or rebut, what the other might say. And, quite likely, the writer of the account might not even have been aware that there was another side to the story. As we say in journalism: Consider the source.

To get a balanced view of what really happened, use this trick of creative research: Find every account you can find. Compare them. Try to understand all the witnesses well enough as human beings that you can see why they would be motivated to relate the event in the ways they did. But also keep in mind that they likely believed their versions of the story, because they didn't live long enough to read the history books that eventually got near the objective truth.

On the other hand, consider this incident: In October of 1813, a warrior named Shawano gave his eyewitness description of Chief Tecumseh's death in the Battle of the Thames. Interviewed again as an old man decades later, he had changed his story completely. Shawano had learned to read, and his new version of the tragedy was the one he had read in books and papers, not the one he had seen with his own eyes. Even eyewitnesses can get their facts wrong.

BOOKS BY BUFFS

Besides the history books, the other novels, and the old documents, your research should lead you to one more valuable kind of written resource, which I call "Books by Buffs." In any field of knowledge, no matter how esoteric, there are single-minded people—"buffs," as they're called, often expert amateurs—who study the details of their specialties and write about them in articles and books. You can think of such people as the baseball card collectors of history. You have to marvel at their near-obsession with such narrow subjects. But they can be useful to you as you research your historical novel, because they do the kind of minute, accurate research you don't have either the time or the inclination to do. Anything you might look up in the encyclopedia, they can tell you ten times as much about it. And most of them are eager to share their knowledge with anybody who shows an interest.

To get a balanced view of what really happened, use this trick of creative research: Find every account you can find. Compare them. Try to understand all the witnesses well enough as human beings that you can see why they would be motivated to relate the event in the ways they did.

I'm speaking here of people who are experts on, say, the uniforms of Napoleon's soldiers; the kilts of Scots Highlanders; the use and history of the bayonet; the varieties of medieval body armor; hygiene in seventeenth-century Belgium; methods and logistics of feeding armies on the march or in winter bivouacs; the prevention of scurvy on long sea voyages; the manufacture and use of wampum; techniques of midwifery in such-and-such a century; cooperage and the tools of barrel-making; the canoe routes and cargoes of the French Canadian fur trade; ingredients used to make ink; amputation, cauterization, and suturing practices of surgeons in Her Majesty's Royal Navy; the latrines of Ancient Rome;

CRUEL AND UNUSUAL

When you find yourself thinking the world can't get much worse, pause and think how much worse some things used to be. You need to know.

In the periods of your historical novels, lawbreakers, even mere rulebreakers, were pilloried, flogged, stoned, decapitated, and drawn-and-quartered as public spectacles. Families could, and did, take the kiddies downtown to watch hangings. In old Roman times, you could watch gladiators fight to the death in the Coliseum, or go there to watch lions devour Christians. A sight-seeing trip along all those roads that led to Rome might include checking out the crucifixions, which on some routes were as prevalent as today's billboards.

Later, there was the Inquisition, in which blacksmiths and mechanics were kept busy making thumbscrews, racks, spiked collars, branding irons, and other diabolical devices for inflicting excruciating pain on heretics.

American army and navy officers used to "discipline" their own troops with procedures you'd see in Abu Ghraib: bind them in stress positions a day at a time in extreme heat and cold; set them astraddle a sharp rail with weights chained to their ankles; dehydrate and starve them; whip them with the flat of a sword; and inflict humiliating and vicious verbal abuse—often for nothing more than failing to salute. For sleeping on post or desertion, punishments ranged from bloody whippings to branding or hanging; the beloved George Washington himself put soldiers in front of the firing squad for mutiny.

There's no end of examples of man's inhumanity to man, as your protagonist is likely to observe and consider whenever he might entertain a notion of defying authority. Research to learn how cruelty and fear were used to control people, back in "the good old days." Your protagonist will have reason to keep such things in mind.

the history of harness-making; siege weaponry from catapult to cannon; uniform buttons and ice-creepers excavated from French and Indian War battle sites; packing and shipment of buffalo hides; spear-hunting with the atlatl; composite bows of the Mongol archers; mussel-eaters of the riparian tribes in pre-Columbian America; farming and herding practices of the Vikings ... and so on.

Almost everything that ever was made or used at any time in history or prehistory has been collected, studied, and written about by scientists or dedicated hobbyists, and their articles and books abound in libraries, bookstores, and museums. Many of those publications are illustrated by drawings or photographs. Often, such writers put the details in historical context and tell pertinent tales, but these aren't really history books in the general sense. Very often these are the reference books used by period re-enactors, or "living historians," a strange and wonderful breed of folks whom I'll discuss later in this chapter.

REPRINTS

Some small specialty publishing houses are in the business of reissuing out-of-print books that have value as historical references. These books might be of broader interest than the "books by buffs" mentioned above. Heritage Books in Maryland in 1990 reissued, for example, a 1906 volume called *Americans of 1776: Daily Life in Revolutionary America*, written by a Boston University professor named James Schouler (now long dead), which covers everything from laws and customs to farming, trade, printing and journalism, manufacturing, literature, education, religion, politics and entertainment, dress, diet, medicine, the practicalities of land and sea travel, disease and philanthropy, finance, and crimes and punishments. A section on boozing, for instance, cites a Boston gazette that listed eighty phrases current in 1771 "to denote a good fellow who is more or less under alcoholic influence." Those phrases would be good to draw from when you're writing a scene.

Another Heritage classic reprint, one of particular value in gleaning descriptions of domestic life and manners, is *Customs and Fashions in Old New England*, by Alice Morse Earle, first published in 1893. This is a trove of archaic facts about the mundane matters of life, written by a woman with a rich vocabulary. As a horseman, I delighted in this description of a particular old mare:

> She was a villainously ugly animal of faded, sunburnt sorrel color. She was so abnormally broad-backed and broad-bodied that a male rider who sat astride her was forced to stick his legs out at a most awkward and ridiculous angle ... Being extremely short-legged this treasured relic was unprecedentedly slow.

She continues, "Being so wide, though, that old mare was perfect for carrying a pillion or side-saddle, making her an ideal vehicle for a woman—or for a couple, with the woman mounted behind her husband." (This must be the Harley-Davidson couple of that age.)

These are only two examples of the kinds of reference books out there worth the search. Such reissued volumes are distributed in museum gift shops and historical society bookstores, and advertised in historical and antique periodicals, as well as in independent bookstores and online booksellers. I won't go into listing such books or publishers, as an entire tome could be compiled. And there are dozens of specialty publishers who keep producing these printed reliquaries. All I need to do is point out that anything you imagine you need to know about the past is there, somewhere, and as you look for it you'll find there's a hundred times that much that you didn't even imagine you'd need to know.

Those authors, working when it was "now," describing and compiling what they knew had been "then," are among those whose shoulders we stand on as we teach ourselves to teach our readers.

One of the most pleasant rewards of the historical novelist's trade is in this world of practical archaism—not just the pleasure of finding out about some object or method that will help you make your story more vivid and believable, but in the enthusiasm of those who amass such information. And here's a tip: If you find some obsolete device or tool that will be used in your story, learn how to use it.

Say, for example, the intriguingly named foot adze, a tool used in hewing logs for most of the cabins and barns made in frontier America. I knew that if someday I would be writing a scene in which someone is building a log house, I should know how to describe the use of the tool, to make the scene vivid, and instructive, too. So I learned to use it, and built part of my log home with it. I was lucky enough, or skillful enough, that I still have all my toes. Many a frontier carpenter didn't.

Or consider the quaint white clay tavern pipe that you see being smoked in many old paintings. That curved stem might have been as long as the smoker's forearm. Was that because his doctor advised him "stay away from tobacco?" No, it was because the pipes were furnished by innkeepers, and if some fastidious lodger didn't want to put his lips where a previous smoker had put his, an inch could be broken off the contaminated end. Which reminds me: Maybe I shouldn't mention one other curious use of the tavern pipe, but I hate to see my research go to waste: There was a time in medical history when doctors believed that certain maladies of the bowels could be relieved by tobacco smoke enemas.

Treat yourself to that image. Maybe even use it in a novel. I did.

BORN TOO LATE

In the United States live tens of thousands of men and women who can't fully abide in the present. So, they get out of it whenever they can and go visit in historical periods of their choice, from the Middle Ages to the Wild West. I mean they go there not just in fantasy, by reading history and watching old movies, but physically. They usually don't go into the past alone, but in groups of like-minded time travelers. What they love, they share: the past.

I've known many of those folks for years, and one thing I've heard most of them say, in a wistful way, is, "I was born too late." Their hearts are in older times.

Such groups hold campouts, bivouacs, and rustic fairs, and call themselves by imaginative names: Buck Creek Muzzleloaders. The Tomahawks. Wetzel's Brigade. Or they bear the names of historic military units whose battles they reenact. Now and then a company or battalion of them gets a role in a movie, because they already know the drill and the tactics, and they are already equipped.

These folks are generally known by the generic term re-enactors. They dress in carefully-researched, usually hand-sewn replicas of period dress; carry authentic utensils, tools, and weapons; and even talk like the old-time people they're portraying. It may be startling to hear it said, but they're in the same business as we who write history and historical fiction: They try to make the past live, vividly enough so that modern people can see and feel as if they're actually there.

Many of those who reenact medieval times call themselves The Society for Creative Anachronism. They dress in the suits of armor and chain mail and gowns and weskits and codpieces of the Middle Ages, and stage great "Faires," including jousting tournaments, archery contests, and feasts where they can eat meat with their fingers. They don't relive the Middle Ages because of a belief that those were "the good old days"—few people have any such illusions about the Middle Ages—but because they are students of that era, and they like to teach modern people about those times by showing exactly what life was like then.

Popular reenactment categories in the U.S. and Canada are colonial and frontier life, the Civil War, and western history and mountain men, but there are festivals and events that incorporate and overlap them, such as Scottish Highland Games and Indian powwows.

Some re-enactors grow famous, like Hal Holbrook, portrayer of Lincoln and Twain. Some are part-time professionals and regional portrayers, such as Kentucky scholar Mel Hankla, who performs soliloquies in the roles of George Rogers Clark and Simon Kenton, dramatic and well-written stage performances. Others are wide-ranging re-enactors such as Thomas Jefferson portrayers Patrick Lee and Clay Jenkinson.

The thousands of others, though, seldom take center stage, but instead participate in group reenactments like battles, trade fairs, and craft shows, or as "living history" inhabitants of reconstructed forts and towns. At least part of the time, these people live in other centuries.

Sense of place is very important, and you can't experience that by just sitting at your computer. Get off your keyboard and do some research that requires you to experience history physically.

A historical novelist is likely to get involved with many of these wonderful chronological misfits, and it can be a nice symbiosis. We historical writers and those re-enactors do our research in similar ways, and we all keep an eye on each other, either to share knowledge or to nitpick at each other, or both.

I knew nothing about re-enactors when I researched my first historical novel, and, thus, didn't consult with any of them. But when *Long Knife* was published in 1979, the bicentennial of George Rogers Clark's victory at Vincennes, re-enactors came out from behind every tree, and I've been surrounded by them ever since. Every historical novel I've written since that one has been informed and enriched by their detailed knowledge of the old times, by their familiarity with everything our pioneer forebears wore, used, made, ate, and did. It was my good fortune that my novel both lauded one of their favorite heroes and satisfied their criteria for authenticity, and they are now among my most avid fans and volunteer advisors. I probably spend more of my public life among people in three-cornered hats, buckskins, moccasins, loincloths, and butternut-dyed hunting frocks than suits, sweats, and Nikes.

These people decide whom they're going to portray and then become those persons from the past, in dress, mannerisms, language, and behavior. Some want to be the soldiers or Indian fighters, some the coureurs de bois, some the Pilgrims, some the merchants and traders and dandies, some the long hunters and mountain men, some the "half-breeds," some the blacksmiths and craftsmen, some the battlefield surgeons, some the scoundrels and trollops. Groups of those individual portrayers might work together to create a band of pioneers, or a community of camp followers—those hordes of laundresses, vendors, sutlers, bootleggers, cattle drivers, teamsters, soldiers' wives or whores that accompanied moving armies throughout history. Those in the wake of the American armies advancing into Mexico in the Mexican-American War in the 1840s were a raffish and picturesque crowd of opportunists and entrepreneurs sometimes referred to by the troops as "Little America." Their makeup and ways are vividly portrayed by novelist Lucia St. Clair Robson in her book *Fearless*, based on the legendary adventures of laundress and sometime battlefield nurse Sarah Bowman. Where my stories and Lucia's overlap—as they did in the Mexican-American

War—I never find errors of fact. I often recommend her books to re-enactors, as well as general readers, because she does what we all try to do: make the past live.

Though I'm not a re-enactor myself, strictly speaking, I'm required to dress authentically enough to stay in their camps when I sell my novels at their gatherings. They have given me, sold me, or swapped for my books, enough eighteenth century shirts, boots, sashes, knives, powder horns, muzzle-loaders, and gaiters that I can go among them without being an anachronism. In fact, lately I've done a little of the Hal Holbrook thing: Sometimes when I give historical speeches, I can step to the podium in my trappings and say, with conviction, "This is probably just about the way my Scots immigrant great-great-great-grandfather Joseph Thom was dressed when he fought in the Pennsylvania militia at the Battle of the Brandywine." It's a natural enough thing for someone like me, who has always felt immersed in the River of History.

Re-enactors are individuals, from all walks of life, so I wouldn't generalize about their motivations or states of mind. But I do know that almost all of them strive for authenticity, and whether they've ever uttered the word "verisimilitude" or not, they pursue it. They help each other achieve it. They explain patiently to anyone who asks questions. They share reference books, and recommend tailors and gunsmiths and craftsmen. Many have become good craftsmen themselves in their quest to get something made just right and make it fit. And they're always appraising. I've often watched as their critically keen eyes go to someone who really looks the part, and in those eyes there will be admiration, but also, maybe, envy.

Some of them are almost fanatic about authenticity. One year in a Midwestern encampment, a fellow brought to the site an aluminum and plastic chaise longue to relax on. He was literally run out of camp, but only after the group humiliated him by twisting his anachronistic modern chair into a knot and running it up to the top of the camp flagpole.

Schedules, places, and requirements of re-enactments can be found easily in special-interest periodicals such as *Muzzleblasts*, *Smoke & Fire News, Scottish Life, True West*, etc., and on their Web sites. And these aren't just American phenomena. England and mainland Europe host many such historical gatherings.

GHOSTS IN CAMP

One problem many re-enactors have is that they are, to put it diplomatically, better fed and more sedentary than the people they portray; therefore, a portly Tennessee truck driver or tax accountant has difficulty looking quite like the half-starved, unbathed, bone-weary Johnny Reb infantryman he is avidly portraying in a battle pageant. But his research has given him the ideal self-image, and that image lives in his mind.

The most perceptive and ironic insight into the re-enactor's mindset I ever read was an early scene in Sharyn McCrumb's novel *Ghost Riders*. Members of a Confederate reenactment unit, camped on the site of the battle they're going to reenact the next day, look up from their cooking fire and see a figure so authentic-looking in his threadbare gray uniform, so gaunt and haggard, that they're awed. When he asks them if they know where another unit is encamped, his accent and idioms are so right, they're all thinking enviously, "Man, this guy has got it down pat! Who is he? Where'd he get that great kit? Wow!"

What they don't know yet is that the spooky guy they're admiring and envying so wistfully is the ghost of a soldier killed on that battlefield more than 130 years earlier, in the battle they'll be acting out the next day.

Any time I get to thinking I'm pretty good at playing meaning-fully with time, I just look at that scene, and grin and shake my head. Any re-enactor reading it would shiver with self-recognition.

Play-actors envying a dead man his authenticity? That, my friends, is playing God with time!

And here's an eerie thought: Maybe I'm occasionally "inhab-ited" by the ghost of Joseph Thom, my ancestor. Maybe I picked him up when I visited his grave a few years ago. I'd never dressed up like him before then.

HISTORICAL NOVELIST MEETS HOLLYWOOD

Film directors are delighted to find ready-made units of re-enactors who can populate a settlement or stage a battle, so you've probably seen some of my time-traveling friends, both Native American and "paleface," on the movie or TV screen. Thereby hangs a droll tale which has some lessons for the histor-ical novelist—lessons about research, authenticity, and the God-like power of authorship.

In 1994, Ted Turner was making a TV film of my novel *Pan-ther in the Sky*, about the Shawnee war chieftain Tecumseh. Among the major battles in which Tecumseh distinguished himself was one fought by a confederacy of Indians against General "Mad Anthony" Wayne in 1794 on the banks of the Maumee River in what is now Northwest Ohio. It's known as "The Battle of Fallen Timbers," because the Indians fortified themselves in a tangle of downed trees left by a tornado.

Turner's movie people had decided to make the whole film in North Carolina because of that state's accommodating state film bureau, and also because of the presence nearby of a Cherokee Indian community that could provide "extras" as warriors in the battle scenes. The set was prepared in the woods beside a lake which was supposed to represent the Maumee River.

One of General Wayne's infantry units in the battle was to be portrayed by a well-trained company of re-enactors commanded by my old friend Dave McBeth of Corydon, Indiana. Dave was a stickler for accuracy, a student of that battle and of others of the period. His unit had trained according in the drills and tactics of old Mad Anthony himself.

American Indian actors playing key roles in the movie were an eclectic bunch of individuals from fifteen different tribal back-grounds, hardly any of them Tecumseh's people, the Shawnees. When the filmmakers sent to the Cherokee reservation for a "cat-tle call" of warriors to do the big battle scene, they were informed that most of the able-bodied young men were already taken: They were miles away on another North Carolina movie set, playing Shawnees in the Hallmark filming of another of my novels, *Follow the River*. (That kind of coincidence sounds like bad fiction, but that's what happened.) What Turner's film crew had to do about its warrior shortage, therefore, was send out to Oklahoma and re-cruit busloads of real Shawnees to play Shawnees in the Tecumseh film: some unintended authenticity.

That was the situation when my wife Dark Rain and I drove to visit the shooting site as guests of the producer, and we arrived on the evening before the big Battle of Fallen Timbers scene was to be filmed. We were escorted down to the battlefield beside the lake, where tree limbs had been cut down and strewn about to simulate the fallen trees. "Here the Indians will be lying in ambush," the producer said. "Wayne's soldiers will come marching up the shore from that direction, the Indians will open fire, and it'll develop into hand-to-hand combat ...."

My headful of meticulously researched details immediately went into alarm mode.

"Whoa! Wait," I protested. "You've got the attack headed the wrong direction! Wayne's army came down the Maumee with the river on his right flank. You've got the water on his left flank!" I was thankful that I'd arrived in the nick of time to prevent a blatant misrepresentation of a major American battle. "You need to have the warriors facing the other way, and bring the army down from up there," I elaborated, pointing this way and that.

I expected the producer to be overjoyed that I'd saved him from an embarrassing error. Instead, he shrugged, waved his hand and said, "Nah. The fighting's already been choreographed. Too late to be changing things around. We film the battle in the morning."

That was one of my early lessons about Hollywood and history. Historical accuracy isn't welcome if it's inconvenient.

When Wayne's blue-coated soldiers and the war-painted Shawnees assembled the next morning on the lakeshore to reenact the battle that broke down Indian resistance east of the Mississippi, there was tension in the air. I got my first sight of Dave McBeth at the head of his troops, and he didn't look any happier than I was about attacking in the wrong direction.

The Indians knew, from history and from the screenplay, that they were supposed to lose the battle. But for them in that moment, 1794 was NOW. Maybe some genetic flashback happened, but when Wayne's troops came charging into the woods with muzzle blasts and bayonets, those unrehearsed Shawnee warrior-actors swarmed over them so ferociously that it looked as if history were about to be reversed on the spot—that not only the battle was backward, but the historical outcome might be, too. A couple of Dave McBeth's bruised and panting re-enactors told me after the scene was over that they thought they might die. Even rubber war clubs can hurt.

Years later, Dave McBeth and I were on the telephone reminiscing about such things. We talked about the hours of solitary study and activity we put into making the past as vivid and true as we can. "You and I are doing the same work," I said, "trying to help modern people hear and see, smell, taste, and feel the formative years of our country. I do it with words, and you guys do it with your physical selves."

"People believe us," he replied. "They trust what you write and what we act out, and they learn. They say they felt like were there."

"And we both love to hear those words," I said.

Here's the lesson of that movie story: The author alone at his typewriter has full autonomy, even if he's relying on the advice and research of others. If he needs a thousand Shawnee warriors to fight in a battle, he doesn't have to send buses to a reservation; he creates them by envisioning them and writing about them. A re-enactor, whether he's Hal Holbrook or Dave McBeth, likewise is the "author" of the personage he portrays, down to the last gesture and mannerism he practices in the mirror.

But a movie maker can't create alone. He needs big, costly teams of creative people and technicians, and the bigger the production, the harder to control the creation. Even the director of a multi-million-dollar movie can't control everything. I saw scenes held up for hours because jet planes from a North Carolina airport kept roaring over, and whole panoramic camera angles ruined because the sky was crossed by jet contrails. Then there's weather. And, of course, there was that decision that it would cost too much to restage a history-shaping battle scene and do it right.

You the novelist can re-create accurately the whole uproar, horror, and consequence of the battle, for the price of a typewriter ribbon or a printer cartridge. You have more perfect Godlike creative power than Steven Spielberg or Cecil B. DeMille. How does that make you feel?

ON SITE

In addition to re-enactors portraying their forebears, there are places that portray their old selves: historical sites and museums, preserved buildings and battlefields. Go to them when you can. Many such places are exact replicas of the forts, camps and settlements you'll be writing about. Many are maintained by national or state park services, or by local historical societies. The rangers and curators are usually as passionate and dedicated to the sites as re-enactors are to their characters. Some historical sites, in fact, employ re-enactors full-time or part-time, to talk to tourists and school groups, to demonstrate old-style blacksmithing, spinning and weaving, crafting and soldiering as "living history."

And many such places are staffed by historical scholars of renown. In such places, you can get not just research information but the invaluable sense of place that is an ingredient of good historical fiction.

And some of those places are haunted. (Don't snort.) One such haunted place is, of course, Gettysburg Battlefield, for obvious reasons. Another is the Wilderness Battlefield in Virginia, where my wife and I both saw a tattered ghost pass outside the window at dusk while we were dining with old friends who live there. It's a place where wounded soldiers lying on the ground burned to death one night when the undergrowth caught fire. And then there's Fallen Timbers, up beside the Maumee in Ohio. Not the movie site in North Carolina, but the real place.

Yah-ma Shepard, a Shawnee Indian friend of mine who is an ex-Marine, a truck driver, used to tell me about a recurring dream he had often of lying on the ground behind a log and being horribly, painfully killed in the midst of a terrible uproar.

Driving his rig along U.S. 24 near Toledo one day, he began to hear the familiar din of that recurrent dream, and felt a strange,

thrilling dread. He pulled onto a parking apron in a park-like setting. Led by some awful compulsion, he got out of his truck cab
and walked downslope toward the river. He saw a big rock memo-
rial that said a chief named Turkey Foot had been killed there. It
was the Fallen Timbers battleground. As Yah-ma walked down the
slope, the uproar in his head grew so loud and fearsome and painful, he clapped his hands over his ears and ran back to his truck.

'I knew then," Yah-ma told me, "that was where I had been
killed. I can't go back there. It's too strong."

Yah-ma's other terrible haunted place is a little historical building in Marietta, Ohio, where American land agents worked long
days to sell parcels of Shawnee homelands to the white men coming down the Ohio River. He told the docent there, "This is the
little room where we died."

Some places, you'll feel the haunting. Go. See. Touch. Learn.
When you really feel it, your research has probably reached that
transcendental stage I mentioned in the beginning.

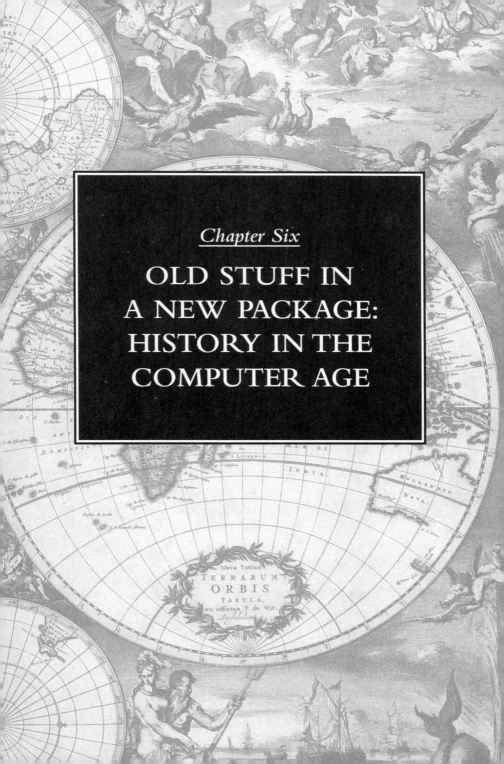

Chapter Six

OLD STUFF IN A NEW PACKAGE: HISTORY IN THE COMPUTER AGE

massive transformation is taking place in the compilation of the human story: the electronic database. The Net. Call it what you will. It's old stuff in a new package.

That the computer, a relatively new technology, is being used to search and store history seems as anachronistic as anything could be. But the computer is a tool, and the use of tools has always been an important theme in the human story, starting with stone implements. Think of the opening scene of the Stanley Kubrick film, *2001: A Space Odyssey*, leaping from Stone Age to HAL, the supercomputer. So far, the computer has been just a tool (though to some, it's almost a god), and like any tool, it will be used differently, to different degrees of efficiency, by different users. You, as a historical researcher and novelist, will adapt it to the particular way you work.

History researchers of my generation had all the information you have, but as I said before, we had to go out at least as far as the library to get it. Now we know the Internet is there, and we hope that we old dogs can learn the new trick.

I've asked several of my peers—historians and historical novelists—how the advent of the computer and the worldwide database has changed their methods of acquiring, verifying, cross-referencing, and storing historical data. These are people who were adept at the old index card systems and now are adapting to computer research. I offer their methods and preferences as possible avenues for your own research.

IN THEIR OWN WORDS

JOHN SUDGEN, ENGLISH HISTORIAN: Dr. Sugden, biographer of Lord Horatio Nelson, has been described by fellow historians as "an absolute mole" for his tireless burrowing in archives. Our paths crossed because we both had written books on the great Shawnee Indian war chief Tecumseh, that key ally of the British against the

Americans in the War of 1812. I asked John if the advent of computer research had changed his methods of acquiring data. His reply:

> Not in any appreciable way. Most of the sources I use are manuscripts, and such manuscripts that it's doubtful anyone will ever put online, at that. I suppose it would depend on the kind of history one writes....I still love handling the original record, and most of the time I don't have a choice.
>
> However, the Web is getting better. Just think of the genealogical data in such records as censuses and registers of births, marriages and deaths that now can now accessed online.

My wife Dark Rain's breakthroughs in genealogical fact-finding attest to that. Missing links that had frustrated her for thirty years were suddenly found and connected when she turned to genealogical research software.

As for storing and cross-referencing, John Sugden said, "With reluctance, I graduated to writing and storing my texts on discs. However, I still file my notes, papers, and source materials in filing cabinets as I've always done."

He'll probably be glad he did. The technology is developing so rapidly that some electronic data storage systems only a few years old are obsolete and can't be read anymore. And paper is more durable than many of the electronic storage devices.

As for the reliability of online data, he said,

> I'm afraid that the quality of so much of the online historical material is poor. I think the veracity has been changed. Misconceptions spread faster. Any history professor will tell you that students are quarrying the Internet rather than books, and suffering thereby. A professorial colleague of mine told me he recognizes the same content coming up in essay after essay, all trawled off the Net. It has become a shortcut for students, but ... it isn't an effective substitute.

> *I'm afraid that the quality of so much of the online histori-*
> *cal material is poor. I think the veracity has been changed.*
> *Misconceptions spread faster.*
>
> —JOHN SUDGEN

JAMES P. RONDA, HISTORIAN: When Western American historian James P. Ronda and I met on the Lewis and Clark Trail, we
soon realized that we had been on parallel paths a long time already. I had researched the life of William Clark for years for my
novels; Jim Ronda was working on an eagerly-awaited biography
of him. I had been researching among American Indians for two
decades and writing novels about them. He had written the perceptive *Lewis and Clark Among the Indians*, which prepared thousands of Bicentennial participants to understand the explorers' often baffling accounts of their encounters with Indian tribes. We
both know you can't research by smoke signals, so I asked him
how the computer has affected his researching and data storing
techniques. He responded:

> I'm not much on using the Internet, but I have occasionally found
> materials on the Library of Congress's American Memory Web
> site to be valuable. Most recently, in doing research for a study
> of fur trade communities, I needed access to a large number of
> archaeological site reports that the National Park Service did on
> Fort Union. The NPS office in Lincoln sent me all that material
> on several disks. ... I hate reading things on a screen, but that was
> the only way to do it efficiently. I still take notes longhand and on
> cards, not on the computer.

I then asked his opinion on the veracity of the new electronic database. "If 'veracity' is defined as 'stability,' then I do have some real

concerns," he replied. "Computer program platforms and Web sites come and go. What is on the Web today may be gone tomorrow, or it may be altered without any clue to such alternation."

He continued:

> I spend a lot of time in contact with literary scholars in various special collections. They're deeply concerned about the stability of literary texts, and therefore resist putting manuscript collections on the Web. ... I know that storage and retrieval is attractive to library folks pressed for space. However, pixels and binary codes are by their very nature unstable and susceptible to either alteration or loss. Let's be very careful here. As Moses learned, there is no substitute for hard copy!

HOWARD ZINN, HISTORIAN: The late Howard Zinn was well into his eighties at the time I interviewed him, but had kept up with the new technologies. He said the computer made it easier for him to gain or check up on material he formerly would have looked up in the library, but that's mostly such facts as names and dates. He told me:

> Sometimes I learn things on the Internet that I didn't know, and I'm getting it faster. But Internet data needs to be verified more scrupulously than data acquired in books. Checking up on the veracity has been made more difficult with electronically acquired data, because very often you don't get the source of the data, and it's crucial to know the source in order to decide how much you trust the information.

So we see again that professional historians put much faith in the reputations of their peers.

DAYTON DUNCAN, HISTORIAN AND SCREENWRITER: Dayton Duncan echoed this dependence on trusted colleagues. He explained:

> I use the Internet to make quick searches, but not for verifying data, also, I use it frequently to locate hard-to-find books ... this has been a tremendous help ... I think the availability and accessibility of historical information has exploded exponentially due to electronic storage and retrieval. With such a rise in supply, of course, comes an increase in questionable veracity. You still need to check other sources; you still need to use sound judgment.

LANFORD JONES, HISTORIAN: Lanford "Lanny" Jones was entrenched in modern time—he was the editor of *People* magazine—before the Lewis and Clark Bicentennial drew him into the past and made a historian out of him. He researched and authored a compact overview of the expedition titled *The Essential Lewis & Clark.* Later, when he learned that Dr. Jim Ronda had chosen to abandon his Clark biography, Lanny plunged in to fill the gap, covering Clark's long and useful life beyond the expedition that made him famous.

In acquiring historical data, Lanny said:

> I use Google as an initial starting point but not a verifiable source. I don't use the computer for fact-checking. I use only published and footnoted primary sources. I trust only primary sources reproduced online, as by Library of Congress, etc." As for storing and cross-referencing his historical data: "Totally on the hard drive."

GARY MOULTON, DOCUMENTARY EDITOR: One of the most prodigious historical researchers I know doesn't consider himself either a historical author or historical novelist, but he is an eminence among us who are either. Gary Moulton refers to himself as a "documentary editor." He is the creator of the monumental reference work, *The Annotated Journals of Lewis and Clark.* While he is admittedly no fan of historical fiction, most of us who write it are big fans of his. He explained,

In my work as a documentary editor I found that computers made my work much more efficient, and I got into it very early. There was a hope in the profession that the dawn of the computer age would speed the publication of documentary editions, and it was all the rage in the 1980s to get up to date on the latest technology.

That promise hasn't been met for a variety of reasons, one of which is that we now have the resources to check and recheck our work, so there's much more returning to the materials to tweak them. Even though mistakes still get through, we probably have more accurate editions than in the past, but they're not necessarily finished more quickly.

He noted, for instance, that the idiosyncratic spelling in the explorers' journals hampered his ability to use spell check. He added, "So, too, do indexing programs flag under the weight of spelling discrepancies in original manuscripts."

As for the accuracy of online sources, he said, "Historical editors don't normally trust the Internet for annotating their texts, but I do see more and more references to easily verifiable facts being cited to the Web. The explosive use of Wikipedia is an example of generalized knowledge not suitable for professional purposes. I'm one of the first to go there for quick reference to matters outside my profession, but I look to more traditional, verifiable, and reliable sources in my own work."

He, too, expressed the historians' reliance on each other: "In my own field, I know the authors of the works I'm studying, can find something out about their prejudices and opinions, can read reviews of the works, and learn if the work has stood the test of time."

Checking up on the veracity has been made more difficult with electronically acquired data, because very often you don't get the source of the data, and it's crucial to know the source in order to decide how much you trust the information.

—HOWARD ZINN

STEPHENIE AMBROSE TUBBS, HISTORIAN: I never asked Stephen Ambrose about his experience with computers—he was gone before I ever considered the question—but his daughter, Stephenie Ambrose Tubbs, author of the delightful post-bicentennial book *Why Sacagawea Deserves the Day Off and Other Lessons from the Lewis and Clark Trail,* has much the same attitude as the other historians:

> The advent of the computer and the Web has changed my methodology of collecting data, cross-referencing and verifying, but it has not changed my desire to find primary documents and bring them to other readers' attention. I think it has just multiplied my opportunities for access to those documents. I think you must be able to trust your source. Getting to it faster doesn't change that basic fact.

AND, SPEAKING FOR OUR OWN ILK ...

Most historical novelists I know make the same assessments of the value of computers in research as do the nonfiction historians. What they're searching for, though, seems to be more general, and they don't worry very much about which historians are saying what about the "prevailing wisdom."

Historical novelists don't seem inclined to engage in peer review very much.

SHARYN MCCRUMB, AUTHOR OF *NEW YORK TIMES* BESTSELLERS *SHE WALKS THESE HILLS* AND *THE ROSEWOOD CASKET*: Of computer research, Sharyn said, "It has made the more obvious data more easily accessible. I could Google, say, the date of the Battle of Chickamauga, instead of having to look it up. But apart from the obvious, I don't trust online sources." However, she did add a benefit: "What the Internet has done is to make it easy to locate used, out-of-print reference books, and it enables me to order them via credit card from all over the world. That is a great saving of time and energy."

LUCIA ST. CLAIR ROBSON, AUTHOR OF *RIDE THE WIND*: Lucia told me:

> I still do my basic research from the usual hardcopy resources—books, newspapers, journal articles—as well as visiting museums and archives and traveling to the sites important to the story. For rewrites, though, the Internet has been an invaluable aid in finding small bits of information that used to take me days or weeks to track down, like what a water heater looked like in 1913, or what the Nahuatl word for 'grandfather' is.

Lucia keeps an open mind about the Internet and watches it evolve. She noted that it tends to be more current than books, and sometimes even refutes erroneous "facts" in books. She said:

> The German magazine *STERN* did a study of the much-maligned Wikipedia and discovered it's more reliable than hardcopy encyclopedias. The last I heard, Wikipedia had seven million articles in two hundred languages. It's being vetted and monitored more effectively as more users come to depend on it. I like Wikipedia because the articles usually list bibliographies.

And so through the words of these professional historians and novelists we see that every author adapts to new technology or clings to the comfortable old methods in his or her own way, or both. You will do the same. Many who will read this book are probably

RESEARCH CHALLENGE: LONG DISTANCE

In 1847, near the Mexican town of Cerro Gordo, the U.S. Army attacked General Santa Anna's force, which was fortified on a mountain named El Telegrafo, "The Telegraph."

But wait: there was no telegraph line anywhere in Mexico in 1847. Though Samuel Morse had invented a telegraph and a code of dots and dashes, it was not in use anywhere near Mexico. Even the United States had only one short line, in the Washington-Baltimore area, and war news had to be carried by ships and express riders.

Your assignment:

Do some research and explain why a Mexican mountain would be called El Telegrafo at that time.

In our age of instant global communication, e-mail, etc., it's hard to imagine how slow and primitive long-distance communication technologies were, not so long ago: drums, bugles, smoke and fires, flashing mirrors, semaphore flags, post riders and couriers on foot .... In almost any novel, news is an important and often dramatic story factor. Therefore, you will have to research the methods of long-distance communication, in order to tell how it was done then. You don't want to presume, for example, that a transatlantic cable was in place if, in fact, it wasn't yet.

Back to the matter of the telegraph, and another research assignment:

When Abraham Lincoln was assassinated in 1865, the news of his death could have been telegraphed to New Orleans, but it wasn't. Find out why it didn't get there until a steamboat brought newspapers down the Mississippi from Illinois.

***

Your research should have revealed: The word "telegraph"—from Greek "distance + writing"—was in use long before then, being applied to earlier codes such as signal lights.

> The Union Secretary of War forbade telegraphing the assassination news to the South because some Confederate elements were still fighting, after Appomattox, and might hold out longer if they knew Lincoln was dead. The Rebs knew he was for leniency toward them, but expected his vice-president to be severe.

young enough that you've never researched or written anything without a computer. Some of us can hardly bear to look at a computer screen for more than a few minutes. I am one of those old coots myself, and now that publishers insist I submit my stuff electronically, I'm beginning to understand how the dinosaurs felt.

I learned to think with a pencil or pen in my hand, and cursive handwriting is still the way I jump-start my creative juices and initially put prose on paper. I've done so much of my historical writing outdoors in the field that my favorite "laptop" is a loose-leaf notebook with a rainproof leather cover, which needs no electricity, doesn't crash, and never goes obsolete. I've been interviewed a few times by chuckling newspaper and magazine writers doing stories on authors who are so quaint that we still write drafts with a pen. Now and then I'm asked about the rumor that I make my own quill pens and write all my first drafts in ink I make myself out of walnut-hull squeezings or blackberry juice.

That was a myth some newspaper or magazine writer started long ago. It's true that I have made quill pens and ink and learned to use them, as research, and could do it now in an emergency, but I sure don't ever want to have to squeeze enough walnut hulls to write a 200,000-word draft of a historical novel.

I don't know how that old false story hangs on so long and keeps coming back. People keep feeding it back into the Internet as a "fact," I guess.

I do wish Wikipedia would stop saying Dark Rain is my fifth wife. I've told them a million times not to exaggerate.

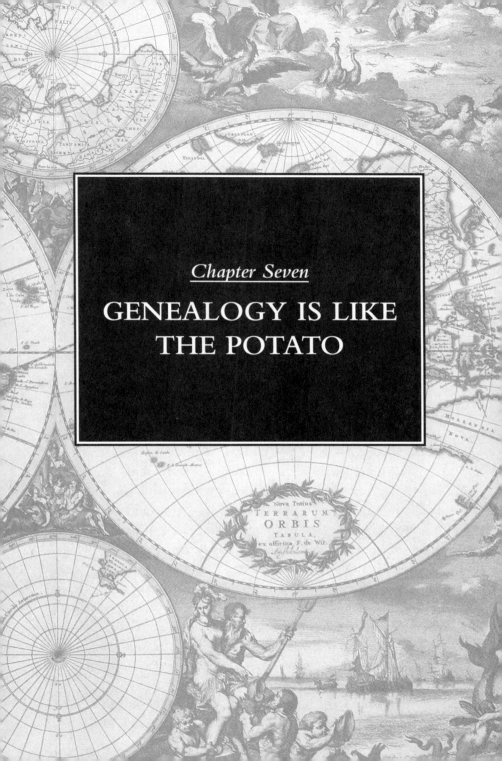

Chapter Seven

GENEALOGY IS LIKE THE POTATO

A n old joke was: Genealogy is like the potato. The best part is underground. (In the grave, that is.)

Historical research likewise. The people we historians and historical novelists want to write about were buried long ago, and, with our research, we go digging them up like spuds.

Genealogy actually *is* history. It's specifically the history of families. Most people researching in genealogical records are trying to learn about their own families—thus about themselves—and usually they're hoping to find someone in whom they can take pride. Many hope to find someone classy, heroic, or titled. (If there's nothing back there but a horse thief, they'll shrug and settle for that. Notoriety is more interesting than respectability, anyway.)

Chances are that you, as a historical novelist, will now and then be doing some genealogical research, not on your own family, but on the family trees of the historical characters in your novels. Even if you don't really have to, do it anyway. You'll almost certainly be glad you did. The more you know about a character's family, the more confident you'll be in portraying that character, and the closer you'll likely get to the truth.

As I mentioned earlier, the woman I'm married to is a veteran genealogical researcher. Much of her life she has been the main family historian, keeping track of relatives close and distant, on both her mother's and her father's sides. Her genealogical work has been especially challenging, because she has American Indian ancestors on both sides of the family. Many families do have Indian ancestors but just don't know it; there were many generations in which you just didn't want to admit that your great-grandma was an Indian because it meant you were of "mixed blood." Because of such long-time secrecy, Native American genealogy is difficult to trace and is almost a science in itself—

especially if more than one tribe is involved. At least four tribes married among my wife's white ancestors. And some of those white ones were in America when it was still a colony. My wife could spend the rest of her life writing historical novels and never get out of her own family tree!

But first, she has agreed to write a section for this book on genealogical research and provide some of the fascinating and useful knowledge that can be put into the hands of a historical novelist.

In this chapter, permit me to introduce my wife, Dark Rain, Water Panther Clan Mother, East of the River Shawnee Band, who will share some of her very human insights.

DIGGING DIRT

Digging for potatoes? Well said, but maybe you'd dig harder if you're seeking gold. Genealogy is rather like gold mining, and sometimes you unearth pyrite (fool's gold) instead. Researching the stories or legends of your own family often turns up unpleasant surprises.

But if you're a historical novelist, the pyrite of a false story might turn out to be as good as 24-karat gold. Stories usually get better if they have hidden impurities in them, and most families have their share of those.

You might have detected subtle clues about old family secrets: things that aren't discussed but merely insinuated, relatives who are or were not in good standing with the rest of the family. The most interesting stories often lie unspoken behind tight lips and furtive eyes.

Certain of my relatives would tell me the same stories over and over until they realized I was onto something that they alone might be guarding. One single oldster might keep in the attic some heirloom or other that is the key to a spicy or shameful story among the kinfolks.

CONNECTING THE DOTS

You might have to do detective work to find those intriguing stories. Try to interview the old folks while they're still above ground. Likely an old aunt languishing grumpily in a nursing home will tell secrets that she'd never have revealed when she was still in the bosom of the family. And suddenly you'll begin to understand the clues—the red herrings, the ridiculous evasions, the sarcastic snickers—that you've been getting for years. Then you start connecting the dots.

The more you know about a character's family, the more confident you'll be in portraying that character, and the closer you'll likely get to the truth.

Some family histories are full of gaps left by disappearances, as men went away to sea, to war, to work in the logging industry, to gold rushes, to ride the rails as hoboes in depression times. Some simply couldn't stand their circumstances (or wives) any longer and headed out. Some started new families and never came back. Some intermarried with other races and, instead of dropping out, were shamed out. Some went into military service and deserted. Some came back with secrets: offspring they couldn't admit to, run-ins with the law, aliases. Family stories that once seemed bewildering can make sense if you look at the historical events and the economic circumstances of the times, and combine those circumstances with what you know of your relatives' character traits.

For the contexts of those circumstances, old newspapers can provide a good start. Many old newspapers are no longer published, but historical societies or libraries may keep copies. Expect to spend hours scanning reels of microfilm. They can give you an objective view of the background of family stories. But don't look at just one old newspaper and quit. Keep scanning. Here's a good reason why, taken right out of my own family tree:

One of my male ancestors in Ohio was found one morning in several pieces strewn along a railroad track on a blind curve. The first newspaper item about it was titled, "Unfortunate Accident." The next one, shortly afterward, called it "Suicide." And when his death was next mentioned in the paper, the story was "Biggest Murder Trial in the County." It seems that a couple of local ruffians with a beef against him had found him drunk and put him on the train tracks to sleep it off, with his neck on one rail and his ankles on the other.

Those three stories were in two local newspapers. It was common in those days, a century ago or more, for even a modest-sized town to have two newspapers at least.

Genealogical research in those hardscrabble Ohio hills back then had given me a picture of what my male ancestors there were like, so the third story was the most credible.

Individuals see those events and times through their particular eyes, and modify them by their personal biases and prejudices, or, more generally, as someone in their own social realm would see them. My different family members remembered the demise of my male ancestor in whichever way suited them. Some chose just not to remember it at all, and might say, "Henry who?"

Just as there are gaps in family memory, there are gaps in written records. "The papers were burned in a courthouse fire," is an obstacle that brings many a genealogical researcher to a skidding halt. But don't let that stop you. Almost anything that was recorded in the county seat courthouse records had its counterpart in the records in some other branch of government. Lost census records can throw you for a loop, but tax records can reveal much of the same information. A family Bible or the records of a fraternal order might have a date or a fact that you can't find in military records. There are always alternative places to look, sometimes turning out better information than what you intended to use.

You can start educating yourself in this field by browsing the many fascinating genealogical magazines in the bookstore. Warning: You can get addicted to these!

MEANWHILE, FOLKS LIVED

While drawing your family tree, pay attention to the mundane, practical details of those whose existence you're tracking. It's important that they lived, but what's really interesting is *how* they lived. Much of that is written down somewhere, maybe in diaries or letters.

Are you familiar with hog butchering? Your ancestors were likely up to their elbows in that carnage every year, and butchering is a powerful assault on all the sense and the sensibilities, and this might have informed their writing. In other words: Practice vivid reading. Did your forebears get water right from a spring or a creek, or via a downspout to a rain barrel or a cistern? Or, did they undertake the once-in-a-lifetime ordeal of digging a well? Was there a still on the hill? How many members of a big family could take their Saturday night bath in one tin tub? (All of them.) In what order? (Usually Papa got the water when it was clean and hot, then downward through the sons, with the little girls last). Outhouses figure largely and amusingly in family legends, and some of them were two-holers at least. One might accommodate the entire family of four at one time, having custom-cut holes for them. That's a lot of togetherness.

I own a leopard-skin vest, heirloom from a pistol-packing great-great uncle out West, who one long-ago morning found a leopard blocking his way to the outhouse and couldn't wait for it to leave of its own accord. That would make an exciting and funny scene in a novel, wouldn't it? And speaking of outhouses, I still have steep, wooded acreage where my Shawnee ancestors lived in the hills near Chillicothe, Ohio, an area where rattlesnakes made any trip to the outhouse a matter of life and death. We always took a six-foot forked stick with us in case we had to brush one aside or pin its venomous head to the ground. The rattlers' descendants still reign, though there's no trace left of the facility, or of the Indians.

Life was immediate and sensuous in the old days, before our minds were flooded with blather from all-day radio and television, our senses benumbed by climate-controlled comfort. While you're finding the names and dates for the genealogy chart, don't pass up the human physical or emotional happenings that you'll probably find written down along the way. What's the point of diagramming your family tree if you ignore the spirit and experience of those who are in it?

TIME FLIES

In genealogy, as in general history, time is the measure. But it can be difficult to keep time. Dates can frustrate you something awful. They hardly ever match perfectly. There are many reasons for the discrepancies. Actual wedding dates might be years after a man and woman began to live together as man and wife. "Marrying Sam," the traveling minister, could take two or more years to finish his circuit. By then the couple might have children who attend their actual wedding. By the time someone got around to recording marriages, births, and deaths in the Bible's flyleaf, the dates might have had to be guessed at because no one remembered exactly.

THE UNLETTERED

Illiteracy sometimes was a cause of inaccurate dates and approximate names. In certain times, more people were illiterate than literate—even smart, respectable people. Most American Indians did not have written language at all, so the dates of the events of their lives might be found nowhere, unless the missionaries got hold of them and recorded their conversion to Christianity, christenings, childbirths, transgressions, punishments, and funerals.

Often, illiterate folks would have to pay a scribe or amanuensis to write mail for them. Large proportions of enlisted soldiers couldn't write. If they were away from home for months or years, their families might not know anything about their well-being unless they could get a clerk to write an occasional letter for them. Most officers were literate, but in the military caste system they were above such matters as writing home for their private soldiers—except, perhaps, to report their death by combat or disease.

THE MANY WAYS OF
GETTING IT WRONG

The laws and customs in institutions have varied at different times, and some things we now deem "vital statistics" weren't even recorded. Government documents can be erroneous, having been kept by humans. Much reported information about battles or disasters, for example, might have been reported by survivors whose testimony was confused and one-sided. Depositions might have been written down by someone who was hard of hearing. Or the person dictating the information might have had an unfamiliar accent, a lisp, teeth missing, or a chaw in his cheek. Such things can account for records that seem generally correct in names and dates but show perplexing differences.

No records are perfect. Most professional and government records do cite names of relatives, which aids in verifying identification. Coroners' and morticians' records differ, but may include such information as hair and eye color, complexion, scars, toothlessness, or other noticeable infirmities that can flesh out the image of an ancestor who lived before photography and never sat for a portrait or sketch.

While you're finding the names and dates for the genealogy chart, don't pass up the human physical or emotional happenings that you'll probably find written down along the way. What's the point of diagramming your family tree if you ignore the spirit and experience of those who are in it?

STAND ON THE GROUND

I encourage you to go to the locations of family homesteads. The information you can absorb by an onsite trip can enrich your writing as you experience the way the earth smells—hot and dry, or wet from a rain shower—how the ground feels beneath your feet, the views you get from favorite places, the species of plants and flowers and trees there, the views from the rivers and creeks. All of this can add richness to your story by taking your characters to places where they loved (or maybe hated) living. Environment influences our lives and attitudes, even the ways we experience life and gauge our happiness.

Be aware, though, hardly any place looks quite as it did in decades and centuries past. The natural distribution ranges of plants and animals have shifted, some are now extinct, some crowded out by imported species grown wild. Two centuries ago, coyotes

weren't known east of the Great Plains; now we hear them sere-
nading in the valleys around our Indiana farm. (One female coyote
even volunteered to live at our house and be our varmint extermi-
nator for nine years.) If you write about lovers taking a stroll down
a forest path and picking a flower, be certain that flower did indeed
bloom there in that time. As my husband forewarned me, there is
a nit-picker out there somewhere just waiting to catch you in an
error and let you and the rest of the reading public know about it.
Old diaries, and the reports of naturalists, can tell you what lived
there then.

PLACE NAMES

One other kind of error can arise concerning time and place. You
can make up places in a historical novel, but more likely you'll be
writing about real places. If you write about real settings, remember this: The names of places change, including villages, towns, cities, counties, states, and bodies of water.

At the time of your story, a location might have been known
by a name that a few years later was replaced by some other name.
As America was populated and people moved west, territories became states, and you have to know which they were in whatever
year. State boundaries changed. Some states almost went to war
against each other over boundary disputes. Land treaties and politics kept moving boundaries around. There wasn't a state of West
Virginia, for example, until it separated from Virginia during the
Civil War.

County names can catch you up even more than states. A state
might have comprised three counties originally, which kept di-
viding until it had ninety. What county your story takes place in,
or which one you're searching in for ancestral records, depends
on the year. For example, my family in Ohio is listed as being

residents of Hamilton County because a relative got mail general delivery there. Another record says they were living in Adams County a few years later. Actually they lived farther east, and as the state grew, pieces of land from those early counties, along with others, became known as Ross County. The relatives hardly ever moved more than twenty miles at a time, and sometimes they found themselves with a new county address even though they hadn't moved at all. Worse, when they moved, they might just name the new place after the one they'd left. Sloppy genealogists who only give you a name without the state can cause havoc in your research efforts.

OPENING FAMILY CLOSETS

Some of the skeletons hidden in family closets aren't long, bony ones but chubby baby ones. Genealogical research turns up illegitimate children now and then. Sometimes their existence has been elaborately disguised to save someone's reputation.

How do you recognize illegitimacy when it crops up in your research? Do you even want to recognize it after all this time? What do you do with it? (Think Hippocratic Oath: "First, do no harm.") I've already discussed briefly some of the problems with reporting and validating marriages, but uncovering an actual illegitimate child in a family can be shocking or devastating. Respect the innocents, even if they are already gone. On the other hand, a little bastard can add real zest to the plot of a novel.

Community morals change over time. An unwed mother in certain eras—not all that long ago!—might have felt so disgraced and desperate as to attempt suicide or a self abortion. Now it's not illegal to have an abortion (though there's still powerful "pro-life" pressure exerted against it), nor do single mothers bear such a stigma as in the past.

In more censorious times, events that "didn't quite add up" were merely whispered about and never discussed openly, but explanations had to be held at the ready, and much intrigue and ingenuity were contrived (which probably didn't fool as many as supposed). It sometimes happened that an illegitimacy remained an elaborate secret until the person keeping the family Bible would at last scribble the truth in, fearing God's punishment for lying in the Good Book.

Bastardy has long been at the heart of classic story plots, in novels and on the stage. And bastard children were often keep secret not just because it was scandalous, but often because of legal consequences. In the old days, inheritances usually went to the oldest son. Sometimes it was necessary to specify the oldest legitimate son. That could make a big difference, indeed. It would be presumed that the illegitimate son would have lived away from the family, with no exposure to the family enterprises, nor sense of propriety in the community. On the other hand, the bastard might have grown up to be more noble and deserving than the legitimate heir. The plot variations were almost infinite, say, in Victorian novels. But art imitates life, and any sort of deceit and hanky-panky that made the plot of an imaginative novel might just as well turn up in a real family tree.

All stories include human beings, and human beings are prone to error. If you don't believe me, just dig around in genealogy awhile, and you'll see that, if anything, I've understated the errant side of us all. A respectable father and mother might go along for ten or even twenty years with no new children being born, then suddenly a little one appears under their roof. Such an unexpected "blessing" might secretly be the inconvenient offspring of one of their unmarried daughters, or of a niece, but the couple claim it as their own.

Or it might be that after the marriage went insipid, or the husband developed some difficulty, his wife took a secret lover and got pregnant. A proper explanation would have to be supplied, and in those days they didn't just burst out singing, "Viva Viagra!"

One family in my tree had five children. The middle boy's last name was spelled differently, but when spoken sounded like the others' names. At first, I presumed it a mere spelling error. That is, until I discovered in later research that the husband had gone away for several years and returned to find his wife had a child who was conceived and born in his absence. She explained that his brother was the father of the child, and just imagine the scenes that ensued. Yet, the man kept the child—who was his nephew in a manner of speaking—took care of him, and, in his will, treated him as he did his own children. But his different spelling of the boy's last name was deliberate, probably a lasting reminder to his wife. A story in Daniel Boone's life is similar.

A newlywed couple, as early as four months after the wedding, have a healthy, fully-developed, twelve-pound baby. Amazing! Imagine what a whopper it would have been if it had gestated the usual nine months after the wedding night! Anyone who was paying attention, of course, knew better, and it would remain in the back of their minds; however, by marrying before the child was due, the bride and her family averted the censure that would have been brought upon them by an unwed mother. Such were the measures taken to keep names out of the mud.

MISCEGENATION

Race is one of the great and terrible undercurrents in the river of American history, and among slaveholding families, miscegenation was easier done than said.

Because of our long involvement with the Lewis and Clark saga, and Virginia history in general, my husband and I were usually within musing range of Thomas Jefferson and Monticello. The matter of Jefferson's intimacy with his slave Sally Hemings is always buzzing, and it rose to a roar a few times in recent years, with much-publicized discussions involving the relative status of the all-white Jefferson descendants and those with Hemings blood. It has always been so much more than just a plantation scandal, and just about everything that could be said about it has been said, over and over. But one gentleman of the Hemings family asked a rhetorical question a few years ago which, as far as we Thoms are concerned, should make everybody else just shut up about it: "So, then," he said, "are we to believe it's more reprehensible that Mr. Jefferson slept with a black woman than that he *owned* one?"

Although a novel shouldn't be preachy, it might well have a moral, and something like this shows how cogent the moral might be.

MEANWHILE, BACK AT THE SLAVE QUARTERS ...

The genealogist, like the historian, should try to see each person of interest from as many angles as possible. And one of the most probing and canny perspectives of all is the slave's or servant's view of the master: usually not very flattering.

Few slaves were taught to read and write, because their owners knew that literacy is power. But some slaves and ex-slaves did become literate, and they had some choice stories to tell. If you ever intend to write a novel about southern belles and their dashing, chivalric menfolk, don't start writing until you see if there are any such rare diaries, letters, and memoirs written by the servants who had clean up after them or drag their julep-soaked carcasses up those long, winding staircases and put them to bed. Or by the field hands who were whipped "for their own good," or by the slave girls and young women who were comely enough to come to the unwelcome attention of the master's randy sons. Few of us in modern America can even imagine the dreadful, helpless state of mind that exists under such bondage.

Some of your ancestors, like mine, likely were owned, in one way or another, and it would be hard to write truly about that part of the past without some sense of it. A one-dimensional view of something as horrendous as slavery is a disservice to the reader. My husband once told me that he might be the only person in America who considers *Gone With the Wind* a crappy excuse for a novel, because "it's about a mansion minx with PMS having to put up with little annoyances like the Civil War and the Emancipation."

It was commonplace for slave-owner menfolk to breed the women they owned, with little censure. But if the lady of the plantation ever got intimate with a man-slave, there'd be hell to pay. If Scarlett O'Hara delivered a dark baby, the midwife might have to kill the newborn and have it buried before Master Rhett came in from his travels and saw it. An excuse might be invented that it was deformed or stillborn, for the fact was that if the mistress of the manor was suspected of misconduct with a male slave, she was in danger of being murdered by her husband or his relatives. We deplore such things these days as the barbaric "honor slayings" of Muslim societies, but similar crimes have happened here.

Sometimes a female slave or midwife would know that a newborn was the result of incestuous antics and take mercy on the mother by smothering the child in its swaddling-cloths, which became its burial shroud. Dishonorable deeds are sometimes done in the name of honor.

Slavery was as ugly and shameful as anything in America's history, and it debased both the slave and the owners. Down in your family tree there might be either the slave or the master, or maybe both, so there could be stories similar to these. They are the stuff of historical novels, too.

MINING THE COURTHOUSE

The county courthouse can be a mother lode for novel plots. Land settlements, wills, criminal cases, civil cases. Divorces weren't as rare in the "good old days" as we like to imagine.

I am convinced you could write a great novel out of almost any piece of paper in these archives. You may find out what people paid their taxes with; it was not always money. Sometimes they paid in tobacco or corn or corn liquor or hemp—the fabric variety, not the toke kind. As for drug use, you probably won't find many drug cases in the courthouse because there weren't drug laws then. But there was much and varied usage. Opium, cocaine, morphine—many patent medicines and tonics and "elixirs"—were loaded with mind-altering substances. You don't read much about it in the history textbooks, but many painfully wounded veterans of the Civil War came home addicted to morphine, which was just then beginning to be administered by field surgeons.

NO, YOUR GREAT-GRANDMOTHER WAS NOT A CHEROKEE PRINCESS

When it comes to the genealogical "digging up" of your Native American ancestors, you might find that they've been literally dug up already, and their bones might be in some of those thousands of boxes and drawers in the Smithsonian, or in some relic-collector's basement along with arrowheads and pottery shards. This is a very touchy matter with Indians. Our forebears haven't been allowed to rest in peace.

And it's complicated by the fact that in many Indian families, we ourselves tried to keep our heritage hidden, sometimes for reputation's sake, sometimes for safety. The Ku Klux Klan (those "sheetheads," as my husband calls them) often thought Indians had no more an excuse to exist than blacks. Like many leaders of the United States Army at certain times, the KKK thought the only good Indian was a dead one. Many Eastern Indian people who were exiled to Oklahoma chose to identify themselves as "a Baptist, a farmer," not as a Shawnee or a Choctaw.

Within the last generation, having Indian blood has become fashionable; no longer is it something you have to hide. "Indian Pride" began rising with the activism of the controversial American Indian Movement, growing tolerance of racial diversity, and even the influence of popular culture, such as Kevin Costner's hit movie *Dances With Wolves.* Suddenly, people who believed they had Indian blood came swarming out, started attending powwows and seeking genealogical proof of their native heritage. Many such persons (so many it's become a joke among Indian people) say, "All I know for sure is that great-grandma was a Cherokee princess."

Please. Quit looking for that princess. She didn't exist. Tribal people had no royalty. Their government was democracy. Many of the Indian "chiefs" best known for cooperating with the white authorities were not even real chiefs of their tribes, merely good talkers or translators, or someone the colonists thought would tell them what they wanted to know and cooperate better than the actual leaders.

And that imaginary Indian ancestor is most often called a Cherokee because the Cherokee are the most populous nation of Indians today, and it's hard to forget a name you see every day spelled out in chrome on Jeeps. Most other tribes' names—other than a few like Navajo, Comanche, Seminole, Mohawk, Sioux—have just been forgotten. But there were some *five hundred* distinct Indian nations in North America, and your Native American blood, if you really have any, could be from any one, or more, of those who weren't Cherokees.

If nobody in your family is quite sure which tribe it was, your first step is to find out what parts of the country your European ancestors came through, and when. It's easy to find out which tribes

LITTLE LABORERS, LITTLE ADULTS

As a historical novelist, you might have to portray children as something other than darling offspring.

In many periods of history, you would likely see them as unpaid little slaves in mines and factories, as apprentices given to craftsmen by their parents to learn a craft, as beggars sent out on the streets by their own parents, as homeless street urchins learning to live by their wits. Read Charles Dickens' novels for a look at how cheap children's lives were in the "most civilized nation in the world" at certain times.

In the 17th Century, orphans were herded off the London streets and shipped off to work in the colonies. As recently as the 1880s, more than a million children were in the American workforce, according to social historian Howard Zinn. Child labor was good for capitalism, because it swelled the workforce and thus depressed the wages of adult workers. And little children were perfect for dangerous work in tight places where adults couldn't squeeze in.

Even children in more favorable economic conditions weren't always adored and spoiled. In arranged marriages, ruled by caste and class, children often were valued more as marriageable assets or potential family earners than they were from familial love. The selling of daughters into child prostitution was done, or at least allowed, by destitute parents. American Indian children were snatched from their villages and sent away to missionary schools without their parents' knowledge.

Obedient children were more convenient than children who could think for themselves, so brutal discipline was commonplace both in the home and the schools, and many children were raised on fear more than affection. Not all childhood is giggles and snuggles.

Whatever the time and place of your novel, you must read and research deep and wide into the prevailing attitudes toward children. Remember, too, that children are the most vulnerable victims of war. Even now, small boys are conscripted into militias and gangs, and armed with lethal weapons. The grief, deprivation and violence of war twist and stunt their impressionable souls even more than ours. Children's cries are the unheeded voices in the rumble of history. When you write history, you can't omit or misrepresent their lives.

lived in what areas and when they were in contact with which immigrants. That begins leading you to the probable tribe, which is a major step in the tracking. But even that can be confusing. Some tribes had name designations for themselves, while the U.S. Government would instead choose to call them by derogatory names given to them by their enemies. Or sometimes the government would just call them something it would arbitrarily choose, and that would become the official name. And, then, further complications arose with the varied attempts to write down tribal names. You wouldn't think, by looking, that Ojibwa and Chippewa are the same name, but when you pronounce them, you get the idea.

If your ancestry actually is Cherokee, you might have grown up believing you're also part Blackfoot, but you can't quite understand how your Cherokee ancestors, who stayed in the Southeast, could have hooked up with the Blackfeet of the Rocky Mountain region. That confusion stems from the fact that a band of Cherokees had a chief named Blackfoot. There were so many in his band they made at least three villages full, located near each other, and the people in his villages were designated under his name: "Blackfoot's Cherokee."

....

[T]here were some five hundred distinct Indian nations in North America, and your Native American blood, if you really have any, could be from any one, or more, of those who weren't Cherokees.

....

Finding your tribe can also be complicated by the tendency of friendly or allied tribes to live together a while for certain reasons and come to be known by the name of the confederation. A large group of Shawnees in Oklahoma formerly lived under Cherokee government until recently, because of an old arrangement of convenience. They were then called the Loyal or Cherokee Shawnee Then they separated and called themselves "The Shawnee Nation," as if they were the only Shawnee, instead of one of three federally recognized Shawnee groups.

As you see, it can take considerable study just to learn what tribal entity you should be searching for your connection. But it can be done. There are vast writings on the native tribes, their migrations, and their dealings with the government and white colonists.

Once you're pretty sure of the tribe, or the confederation of tribes, that your white ancestor probably married into, you can start looking for names. But you might look in vain for Indian-sounding names. Look for the names in your family tree. As early as the 1600s, many Indians who turned up in written records were given, or took, European first names, and even surnames, because they were easier for the settlers to remember and pronounce than, say, Pepquonnahek—and certainly easier to write. Indian languages had some consonants for whose pronunciation there is no letter in our English alphabet. (Mark Twain suggested that Chingachgo-ok, the name of that heroic fictional Indian made up by James Fen-imore Cooper, must be pronounced "Chicago.") Ask an Indian how his ancestor's almost unintelligible name was spelled, and his correct answer will be, "It wasn't. Indians didn't spell."

There are translations of Indian names that turn up in the old re-cords, though. Michikonogkwa, the famous Miami chief, is promi-nent in the history books as "Little Turtle." The Shawnee chief Ca-tahecassa, who spent some seventy of his 110 years fighting paleface invaders, is remembered in history simply as "Black Hoof."

It's important for you to know that most tribes are matrilineal. If that's a new word for you, get used to it. It means the Indian lin-eage is traced through the mother's side.

I could write a whole book on tracing Native-American gene-alogy (in fact, I'm working on it and may get it done someday), and I won't try to write a detailed how-to, here in the middle of my husband's book on historical fiction. I will say that a good place to start is in your county library, where you can get acquainted with the search techniques, the institutions, and the agencies that have the data. I will recommend two archives famed for good Native-American genealogy: The Newberry Library in Chicago and the Allen County Public Library in Fort Wayne, Indiana.

There are several good software programs tied into vast genea-logical records, and some Indian family data is among them. Some Indian tribes have good records of their tribal rolls, but many are understaffed and underfunded, and may never get around to an-swering your inquiries, even if you send them a self-addressed, stamped envelope. Some tribes don't even want to hear from you, because they figure you're just a wanna-be hoping to become eli-gible for scarce tribal benefits.

United States government agencies dealing with Indians all but make a profession out of losing and misplacing records, because the government owes Indian tribes hundreds of billions of dollars under treaties, for land payments and resource royalties, and the less proof of obligation the better. But there are some able and helpful bureaucrats, and if you're lucky, one of those might receive your inquiry.

Potentially a factor in your Native-American genealogical research, either good or bad, is that long period in which the government gave religious missionary and cult groups major contracts to grab up Indian children, beat the "Indian" out of them, cut their hair, dress them, and educate them for menial jobs in the white man's workforce. Some of those groups kept very detailed records that can be useful in genealogical tracing but also serve as terrible dramas of cultural exploitation and debasement. Entire generations were deliberately purged of their native languages and lore.

Sometimes the whites' pursuit to "tame" Indians backfired. When missionaries taught Indian children to read and write, they inadvertently gave them power to understand the system better, and that made them harder to cheat. Many forcibly-educated Indians were shrewd enough to study law, and an Indian lawyer is one of the best assets any tribe can have.

To further complicate your research, there are about five categories of Indians. Remember, our government hasn't been about sustaining tribes but about getting them to assimilate and dissolve, to get rid of its obligations to them. We Indians call that "paper genocide."

Government agencies don't use the same mathematics we do to determine your Indian Blood quantum. We might calculate that you're 1/8th Cherokee, while they figure you're 1/152nd, and thus not enough Indian to be eligible for what the old treaties promised you. Indian people (who were here first) are the only ethnicity that has to do mathematical fractions on what part of them is racially distinct.

That reminds me of a story my husband likes to tell, about the time when he gave blood at a Red Cross clinic up in North Dakota and afterward was resting beside a fellow who was obviously in from one of the nearby reservations. "Lakota?" Jim asked him.

"Right, bro," the Indian replied.

"You look like a full-blood," Jim complimented him.

"Well, actually, right now I'm a pint low."

Jim learned that day, as he says it, "Once you laugh with an Indian, and not at him, you might as well be one."

UNDERSTANDING TRIBES TODAY

The five tribal categories are:

1. federally recognized
2. state-recognized
3. historic tribes
4. tribal groups
5. associations

Some tribes were federally recognized formerly, but budget-minded congressmen once decided that they were getting along well enough in the white world that they no longer needed government assistance, so they created what was called the "disenfranchised tribes." About fifty-four tribes are still fighting to get their recognition reinstated. If your tribe isn't federally recognized, you and your children are not eligible for any federal programs like health or education. State-recognized tribes range from no financial assistance to getting minor help with health or education, depending on state policy.

Historic tribes are those that are neither federally nor state recognized but comprise remnants: Indian people who stayed behind when their tribes were driven west, or some who returned. Such groups seldom get anything except an occasional grant of the sorts that most nonprofit companies and groups are eligible for.

A basic truth is that treaties were contracts. Bands who refused to sign treaties giving up their land in exchange for benefits were discounted as Indians and no longer have federal recognition. Some of us look at all the government strings attached and just decide it's not worth it. As you research Indian genealogy, you'll run into stories of great leaders who were treated like incompetent children, having to beg for government permission to do simple things on their own property that any white man could just roll up his sleeves and do when he felt like it.

Many politicians suspect that the only reason tribes want federal recognition is so they can open gambling casinos. That is sometimes a motive; it has been one of the few advantages modern Indians ever gained in this country. But there are better motives, and one of them is pride. There are spiritual beliefs and earth-connected values shared by most tribes. Diverse Indian peoples share similar tragic histories of genocide and displacement but still see America as their homeland.

Much genealogical searching for American Indian ancestry is done by, and for, people who have reason to believe that they have Indian blood and want to be sure. Many mixed-blood or assimilated Indian families hid their ancestry so well that their modern descendants virtually have to start from scratch to fill in the generational gaps. Some seekers just simply want to know the truth, but many go on the ancestry quest because they want to become associated with a real tribe or with native kin. Most tribal groups' constitutions require clear and substantial documenta-

tion of ancestral connection, amounting to blood quanta speci-
fied by the groups themselves.

A pitiful irony is that many members of federally recognized
tribes scorn the other categories of Indians—sometimes their
own relatives—as not being valid tribes according to government designations. That is, their "authority" on who's Indian
and who's not is the same white man who scattered us and ruined our homeland in the first place.

If that isn't twisted history, I don't know what is. Maybe
what this country needs is more Native Americans who are historical novelists.

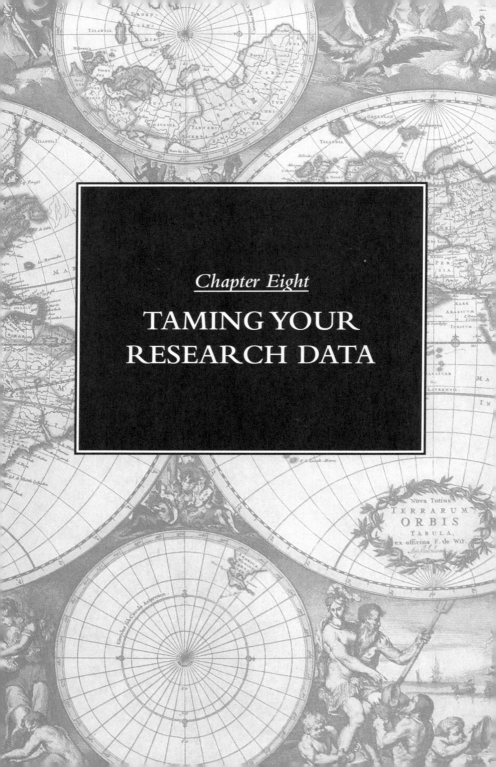

Chapter Eight

TAMING YOUR
RESEARCH DATA

conscientious historical novelist can accumulate so much research data, over so long a period of time, that it becomes like kudzu, a powerful weed.

It can overrun one's mind and work space, and grow so dense and profuse that any part of it is engulfed and obscured by the whole of it.

Like kudzu spreading over tree stumps and up utility poles, it can obfuscate your original ideas and intentions. One good week of research can be so revelatory and intriguing as to seem more interesting and important than your initial concept for the story itself. Or, it can make you forget some other entire area of research you did two months earlier. Even worse (or better), it can disprove what you'd found out before. It's the nature of data to proliferate. And it doesn't accumulate like dead leaves, just piling up. It lives, grows, and changes.

Some writers have the kind of intellect that can correlate and categorize masses of data and recall just what is needed, just when it's needed. Most of us can do that sometimes, but fail at it most of the time. Some of us think we can, but overestimate our minds and memories.

Many modern writers organize their data in their computers, storing and linking the thousands of facts. That is a method which imitates the brain itself, but it's only as good as the programmer.

Others combine computer storage with older filing techniques, like three-by-five cards organized in boxes and trays, or notes kept in hanging folders in filing cabinets.

Veteran historical novelist Lucia St. Clair Robson still uses the system she learned from writing term papers in high school, using four-by-six-inch note cards. She's ready for anything. "My system is simple, adaptable, portable, flexible, available even during power outages, and timeless," she says. She explains:

Over the past thirty years, I've written my books on a typewriter and on a series of computers with three different operating systems. Any information stored on those early machines would have been long gone. Not so my notecards. I keep thousands of them in drawers, two or three drawers of which are assigned to each book. They're filed by subject. I can answer readers' questions about details that I researched decades ago, long before computers became practical for what I do.

A writer well trained in computer applications might dismiss that kind of a system as bulky, dusty, and unnecessary, and perhaps it is these days. But one *zap!* or one instrument gone obsolete or one day of neglecting to backup your data, and that neat little invisible world of data is gone forever. But Lucia will still have all her hard-earned information, and she can read it by candlelight even if the power grid is down.

THE HANDWRITING
IS ON THE WALL

Long before computers were available, I taught myself one way to tame my accumulated data with a simple, dependable, low-tech method: a wall chart. It was made of newsprint sheets pasted together, and measured about 46 x 102 inches, lined vertically and horizontally to make an inked grid. The resulting rectangles were big enough to pencil in notes and references to documents. It covered a thirty-year family saga.

I found it so effective and natural and easy to read that, even if I were now a computer data wizard (I'm not), I would still make a wall chart and use it as my guide. In fact, I have one for the Civil War steamboat novel I'm writing now. This one covers only a couple of weeks of events, hour by hour, but without it up there to glance at and check myself, I could create inconsistencies that might be embarrassing.

I developed that first big wall chart out of necessity after four years of gathering data for my biggest historical novel, *From Sea to Shining Sea*. The research literally had taken me from the Atlantic to the Pacific, and twenty states in between, and my data was in both archival documents and field notes. It covered the exploits and achievements of one generation of the Clark family of Virginia—the six sons and four daughters of John and Ann Rogers Clark. It was a novel built in three movements, similar to the form of a symphony.

The first movement was the Revolutionary War, in which all the sons except the youngest, William, fought and led in decisive campaigns. The second movement was the settlement of Kentucky, a state founded by the second-oldest brother, George Rogers Clark, and whose leading families grew more prominent after the marriages of the four Clark daughters. That movement included episodes of the Indian Wars in the Ohio River Valley. The third movement was the Lewis and Clark expedition to the Pacific, co-captained by William, who had been too young to fight in the Revolution but became the first man to map the vast Great Plains, Rocky Mountains, and Columbia River watershed—thousands of miles of previously uncharted territory. I've already said much about that expedition earlier in this book.

Those brothers and sisters—the battles they fought and the treaties and explorations they made; the frontier dynasty they founded; their comrades-in-arms; their enemies and friends both Native American and white; their slaves—led me to such a mountain of research material in every imaginable form that its organization demanded not just that one huge, general chronological chart, but also a genealogical chart, a double-spread continental map, and enough campaign and battle maps to cover another wall.

That main chronological chart was a grid. Down the left margin ran the timeline, from the novel's first scene in 1773 to the last one in 1806. Across the top margin were column headings with titles covering everything from weather conditions to political developments, from wars to truces, from epidemics to droughts, from military campaigns to legislative assemblies—everything I'd found that had a bearing on the lives of those ten Clark siblings, their parents, offspring, accomplishments, and failures. Thus the big grid on the wall comprised spaces for penciling in not just major events—battles, voyages, treaties, weddings, funerals, epidemics, legislative assemblies, bivouacs, hunting trips, etc.—but also more nuanced details, such as planting seasons and harvests, phases of the moon, holidays, horse races, court trials. In addition, the grid included historical events that were not within the direct narratives of the characters' lives but, perhaps, other events that influenced their lives, such as European wars, treaties and alliances, the Northwest Ordinance, elections, the French Revolution, the Louisiana Purchase, terms of the presidents and the makeup of their cabinets, and the like.

The eldest Clark brother, General Jonathan Clark, kept small pocket journals all through his adult life, in which he recorded each day the weather, where he traveled, visited or camped, what he ate and how it affected his digestion, and any remarkable events such as eclipses, births, illnesses, marriages. All this was written in such tight, small script that a day usually used up only one line. I went through some thirty years of those tedious little booklets, checking places, weather, and incidents against other diaries and reports and memoirs, and now and then verifying something that historians had merely presumed. Many a mundane detail found its way from Jonathan's notebooks to a space somewhere on my master chart. I once rewrote a whole scene because Jonathan's datebook told me it had rained all that day in the vicinity.

Locating such a batch of primary material is like finding treasure. But filing it in usable form was a huge preparatory task. Each notation on the grid had a reference word (more often abbreviation) directing me to the stacks and bundles of research and reference materials, almanacs and censuses along the baseboard under the chart. Literally, the handwriting was on the wall, the footnotes were on the floor.

Some readers are learning the history of their country through the story in my novel. They didn't learn the history very well in school because it was taught in ways that were dry or boring. The historical novelist has a responsibility to keep the history as accurate as research can make it.

Attached to the main chart was an essential little sheet called the Perpetual Calendar, a chart on which one can calculate what day of the week or weekend any calendar date fell on. Sometimes, such a certainty can prevent an error of fact; sometimes it might enhance the verisimilitude of a scene, for example, when a poignant letter penned by a character on a particular date proves to have been written on a Sunday, maybe with a church sermon fresh in mind.

Likewise, an almanac or other astronomical record could tell the author whether there actually was a full moon on the date when a scene occurs. The question might be asked, "Why bother?" The answer might be, "Because of those nitpickers out there who will quit reading you if they find errors."

Another good answer is simply, "Because I want to know everything that can be known that will help me understand the lives and the incidents I'm writing about, whether anyone else ever notices or not."

But one more good reason is this: Some readers are learning the history of their country through the story in my novel. They didn't learn the history very well in school because it was taught in ways that were dry or boring. The historical novelist has a responsibility to keep the history as accurate as research can make it. That's why data storage and accessibility are crucial. There's no better reward than knowing you've done your best. And sometimes you get a bit of good feedback that makes all the effort worthwhile. Let me cite two examples:

Professor Robert Gatten, one-time president of the Lewis and Clark Trail Heritage Foundation, once told me he had searched in vain for the site of a Clark family homestead, and finally found it by reading geographical descriptions in my novel *From Sea to Shining Sea.*

Peyton "Bud" Clark, a great-great-great-grandson of General William Clark, who lives and breathes the family history, has collected many of his ancestors' weapons and accessories. During the length of the Lewis and Clark Bicentennial re-enactment of the voyage, he portrayed his famous ancestor. This was a man who had every reason and resource to be a nitpicker; that was his beloved forebear I had portrayed. By taming my proliferating research, I had made it accurate enough for him. He referred to my novel as "our family Bible. We'd have quizzes on it at dinner." We both have lived so long with his ancestor that we're like brothers now.

If I had met Bud Clark during my research for the novel, I'll bet it would have been even more thorough and accurate. But I didn't meet him until after the book was published, when I was invited to a Clark family reunion in Kentucky.

There's one other reason why I sometimes think I wrote that novel too soon: It would have been so much easier and more detailed if I 'd waited for Dr. Gary Moulton to finish his major opus,

The Annotated Journals of Lewis and Clark, which was published shortly before the Lewis and Clark Bicentennial.

When I started researching the book in 1978, I had never heard of that distinguished scholar. While I was finding and organizing every fact I could find pertaining to the explorers, Gary Moulton was doing the same thing with meticulous skill and great patience under the auspices of the Center for Great Plains Studies at the University of Nebraska. Cross-referencing the journals penned by the explorers and those of four of their enlisted men—and all the subsequent literature relevant to the expedition—Gary completed a multi-volume set of the journals, with thousands of footnotes and a magnificent atlas, that is considered the authoritative record.

How much easier it would have been to get the details right, to understand the causes and effects of certain incidents, and the interrelationships among the men and the tribes they encountered. If only that monumental work had been available as I puttered across America in an aging Volkswagen camper with barely enough money for coffee, food, gasoline, and brandy!

It's not that his finished work would have been a replacement for the Lewis and Clark part of my big wall chart. But such a thorough, well-organized reference work would have sped up the preparation of that chart immeasurably.

Moulton's *Journals* were published too late to help me with my first Lewis and Clark book. But he had tamed and organized so much of that vast body of material by the time I wrote *Sign-Talker* that I was able to "stand on his shoulders" for reference and verification in the preparation of that book.

We have to tame most of our research material ourselves. But there are always people out in the world of historical scholarship who are helping us tame it. It's good to know who those data tamers are. Most authors are relatively solitary folks, not "joiners."

Speaking for myself, I join almost nothing—clubs, alumni groups, social organizations or lodges—but I have had memberships in historical societies and long associations with historical scholars and researchers. Those of us with shared interests in historical subjects are like extended families. We keep each other informed about new research, new books, excursions and programs, and we know that our favorite historical narratives are always being considered and discussed, unforgotten, somewhere out there.

SHIFTING IMAGES

One of the real and constant challenges you'll face in taming your research data is that data isn't dead and inert. It is usually changing and evolving, as I've said, which also means it grows. Much of your accumulated research will subtly contradict other materials you've dug up, and anything heavily studied by historians will gradually change with the evolving "perceived wisdom."

No matter how diligently your colleagues research, or how clearly they write, other able historians are busy somewhere revising the facts and the images. And historians don't like to be out of step with their respected peers.

That's just one more reason why your research material piles up to a nearly unmanageable mass: because there are so many versions of everything.

And you, as a historical novelist, will be judged by the look of the story you put together. Your description of something or someone might have developed from your reading of original documents or your examination of pictures—long since refuted facts that may have "gone out of style" according to later research.

My father, an army doctor, liked to say with a wry smile: "I learned just two truths in medical school. Both of them have been disproved."

YESTERWAR, TOMORRWAR

A friend who was a big-city newspaper editor once sent me the manuscript of a novel he'd written. He is as well read and savvy as anyone I know. But his story made reference to the "Mexican War," and mentioned the infamous Pancho Villa. My erudite friend had confused the 1846 U.S. invasion of Mexico with the Mexican Revolution more than sixty years later.

It's understandable. World history is such a constant succession of wars that it's hard to keep them straight, and the United States has been one of the most aggressive and meddlesome of nations. Yes, we even got involved in that Mexican Revolution. A recent "Isaac Asimov SUPERQUIZ" syndicated in the newspaper mentioned fifteen wars, the United States being involved in eleven of them—nine on foreign soil—and even that list omitted some of ours.

For years I've been making "a modest proposal" that the names of two of the planets in our solar system be swapped. Mars is named for the Roman god of war, but there's never been a war there.

On Earth there has seldom been a year of peace in the whole duration of history. This is the planet that should be called Mars.

The protagonist of your historical novel, even if he doesn't get involved directly in combat, will likely be aware of war, or impending war, or the economic effects of war, nearby or afar. Therefore it behooves you, as his creator, to know all about the wars that involve him or occupy his thoughts. War is, unfortunately, the constant occupation of man, and the source of the mightiest drama. It's hard to ignore it if you're writing about this world, the one we should call Mars.

The phenomena of disproven truths and shifting images affect the accumulated data. They keep adding to it, but you have to keep track of what's old, what's new, and who says so. You have to keep evaluating it, deciding whether to believe this or that, and probably researching it yourself, if something seems to be in doubt.

There were certain accepted "truths" about the Lewis and Clark expedition in the early 1980s when I set out to retrace their route. These were the "perceived wisdom" that most of the historians had pretty much agreed upon; details had been made vivid by writers, painters, and sculptors, and those accepted facts and images colored my portrayal of the great adventure. A few specific examples:

- The name of Captain Lewis's wonderful Newfoundland dog was "Scannon."
- Lewis wore a three-cornered hat, as you could see on all the roadside signs marking their route; Clark wore a furry item of headgear, something like a coonskin cap with no tail, sometimes depicted with a leather bill to shade his eyes. The soldiers wore three-cornered hats or low-crowned slouch hats.
- Sacagawea was usually depicted as a mature, formidable, almost matronly Indian woman with her arm outstretched, pointing the way. Most Americans thought her name was Sacajawea and that she had been the expedition's guide. Her French-Canadian husband Toussaint Charbonneau was portrayed as a lazy, conceited malcontent and a bumbling coward, who looked pretty bad in comparison with the intrepid, forceful Anglo-Americans. (Disparaging Frenchmen is old sport; it didn't start in this century when they tried to talk us out of invading Iraq.)

Starting in the early 1990s, the buildup to the Lewis and Clark Bicentennial brought historians and researchers swarming out of the woodwork, and many of them had been working diligently on modifications of the story, its meanings and its images.

Dozens of new books had been or were being written to coincide with the national publicity for the bicentennial. The Indians were finally getting credit for helping the explorers succeed. Museums were preparing new exhibits, both stationary and traveling versions. By the time the actual three-year observation began in 2003, much of the message and the imagery had been changed in subtle ways.

Many old-timers in the Lewis and Clark Trail Heritage Foundation resisted such change. But historians and history buffs generally like to believe they're in the know; they don't like to be left behind. So most of them considered the new expert evidence and revised their old imagery to fit the new perceived wisdom.

Following are three significant revisions that occurred during the buildup to the bicentennial.

RENAMING THE DOG

Lewis's dog, formerly "Scannon," became "Seaman."

The dog's name had been written down just once, in Lewis's hand, and for many years it was read as "Scannon." In my 1984 novel, I had used that name. I had seen the handwriting myself, and I had no doubt that it was "Scannon." Why that name? One would presume he had already been named when Lewis purchased him at the start of the Ohio River leg of the journey.

But scholar Donald Jackson, compiler of all known correspondence pertaining to the expedition, was very keen on cursive writing, and he averred that the handwriting said "Seaman."

That made a certain kind of sense, as the big, water-loving Newfoundland would be traveling as a sort of four-legged boat crew member, so "Seaman" became his official name. Jackson's sterling reputation made the change easy for folks to swallow. Since half a million copies of my novel were out there in the world with the dog being called "Scannon," I had no choice but to be thought wrong, because the consensus had changed. Though I've spent much of my life reading old cursive, and it still looks like "Scannon" to me, the new reading made sense, so I now think of him as "Seaman." Often, as he was mentioned in the captains' and soldiers' diaries throughout the journey, he was referred to only as "my dog" or "the captain's dog," and never again by name, so there are no more opportunities to judge by scrutinizing handwriting.

....

[O]ur visual images of history are constantly changing, and no historian, aficionado, or historical novelist likes to be left in the dust when the consensus moves on.

....

Incidentally—demonstrating how inventive you can be in historical fiction—among the dozens of historical and fictional books published in connection with the bicentennial, at least three novels for young readers were published in which the point-of-view character or narrator was the dog himself. Being *au courant*, he thought of himself as "Seaman."

But I'll be skeptical until I see it in his own paw-writing.

CHANGING HATS

One of the most striking visual updates of the Lewis and Clark expedition was the new set of hats worn by the two officers and their troops.

The tricorn, or cocked hat with its brim pinned up on three sides, so familiar in all our history books, had traditionally been Lewis's headgear in all the paintings and on the road signs.

But Bob Moore, a National Park Service ranger at the St. Louis Gateway Arch had been doing intensive research on the authorized apparel of the United States Army of that period, and he had enough evidence to start revising the images of the hats well before the observances opened, with the help of a new-generation Lewis and Clark artist, Michael Haynes. Their writings and paintings appeared in *We Proceeded On*, the official periodical of the Lewis and Clark Trail Heritage Foundation, and they made presentations at the conferences.

Captain Lewis's hat would not have been three-cornered, Moore averred. By that time an Army officer would have been wearing a *chapeau de bras*—a tall, black hat shaped like a half-moon, worn with peaks fore and aft at a slight angle from the line of sight. This headgear would have added four or five inches to the apparent height of an officer, more than one wearing a tricorn. Such display was meant for psychological effect on the enemy in the field, as were the towering bearskin shakoes of the British or the cone-shaped, brass-faced hats of the Hessian Grenadiers. Soldiers just looked bigger.

The hats of the expedition's enlisted men also popped up several inches because of Moore's research. Their uniform headgear now became a cylindrical top-hat with a brim, with a strip of black bear fur up over the crown for parade occasions, rather than the low-crown slouch hat or tricorn depicted in the earlier art. Moore's research and Haynes's paintings went on to revise details of the military coats and accoutrements, but the hats were the most striking changes. (As we know from reading the journals, the hard progress of the expedition eventually wore out most apparel, and attire was rags, leather and furs, with fatigue caps, or even with kerchiefs tied around their heads, sometimes even cone-shaped woven hats bought from Indians, and boots replaced by handmade moccasins.)

So the data keep accumulating, and the images keep changing.

WOMAN BECOMES GIRL

Sacagawea was always a misrepresented figure, in one way or another; she's always being revised to suit the fancies of those who imagined her in the context of the story. The same would be true of any historical heroine you'd write about—Cleopatra, Joan of Arc, Mary Magdalene, Mata Hari, your own great-grandma—so this one female member of the famous journey of exploration serves as a lesson that can be applied anywhere in historical writing.

Some historians had aggrandized her as an important guide who pointed out the way for the explorers. Women in literary circles imagined her as a romantic, free spirit, a courageous mother protecting her infant son in the wilderness, a pioneer for women's rights. She was put forward, as you'll see in chapter 12, as the first woman in American history to vote. She was the object of Captain Clark's amorous desire, or she wasn't. She died at a very young age, or at a very old age, depending on which historians or novelists you believe. She was a Shoshone, or was she a Hidatsa?

Those who have seen her statues or her image in murals or on book cover art, would believe she was a mature, glamorous woman. Anyone who remembers an outlandish Hollywood adventure film called *The Far Horizons* might remember her as white actress Donna Reed in a shade of suntan makeup, and such a contentious plot figure that Charlton Heston (Clark) and Fred MacMurray (Lewis) got into a fistfight over her. Nobody takes historic license like Hollywood.

The truth-hungry historians and history buffs wanted to fix a more accurate image of her in time for the bicentennial. It wasn't easy, but one thing they could agree on by testimony in the expedition journals was that she was barely into her teens, and if she was beautiful, no one had bothered to write that down. In real life she might or might not have looked like the Sacagawea on the commemorative dollar coin, which was modeled on a sixteen-year-old Nez Perce girl chosen by the U.S. Mint from an intertribal competition. Sacagawea was even younger than sixteen, and very pregnant, when the explorers hired her husband Charbonneau as an interpreter. He was about three times her age, and she wasn't his only child bride.

She wasn't the expedition's guide, though she did point out a few helpful landmarks when the expedition reached her home territory near the headwaters of the Missouri River. She was a tough, resourceful, often brave and useful, and occasionally strong-willed, young mother, probably more scrawny than shapely. After being almost miraculously reunited with her brother and her tribe near the Great Divide, she didn't stay with them but continued on with the white soldiers, for reasons that will leave storytellers forever speculating. The fact is that for nearly two years she walked, rode, and canoed thousands of miles of rugged country with a company of white men and her middle-aged husband, while carrying and nursing a baby boy. Pick up a Sacagawea dollar (an odd token, considering that she lived in a moneyless world), look at that girlish face, and marvel not just at her, but at women and what they can do.

As for that baby on her back, you can imagine what his first spoken words were: "Are we there yet?"

My point here is that our visual images and interpretations of history are constantly evolving, and no historian, aficionado, or historical novelist likes to be left in the dust when the consensus moves on down the trail. Therefore, keeping the facts and images up to date (even though they're centuries old) is an unending part of taming your research data.

THE AFTERLIFE OF DATA

Well, at least you can stop that endless data management rat race when your novel's finished, right?

No. Better not, until you're all through revising. You'll still need it.

Then, after it's been published, you can forget it, right?

No, even then it's a good idea to keep managing the data.

To think big, here's a reason: Somebody buys the movie rights to your great historical novel, and you might well be asked to consult on facts and details. When that happens, you need to have those details at hand and know where to find them.

Also, a good historical novelist often gets invited to give lectures to history buffs and even to historical societies. When that happens, you need to know what you're talking about, because the people in your audiences likely have studied the details. They have questions to ask. They appreciate you if you know as much as they know. And if you can tell them something they didn't know, and it's correct, you'll have that many more fans. Furthermore, they might well be able to enhance your own knowledge, which of course helps you, and makes them feel really good. There is a wonderful camaraderie between knowledgeable authors and their knowledgeable readers, and that camaraderie is one of the best rewards for knowing your facts and telling your story well.

Here's one more tip from an old hand: You might well accumulate more information than you'll use for a particular novel. But the good thing is that it's there if you decide later to write another novel about similar subjects. Most of the novels I've written have been "spin-offs" from earlier ones I'd already written. So, each time I started, I had that much more research data already at hand. But it had to be tamed and organized so I could find it when I needed it.

The more you know, the better you can write. Be your own library! Hoarded knowledge is like a savings account. It's an asset you can draw on later. Even more simply put: Knowledge is fortune.

And your filing system is your safe deposit box.

Chapter Nine

IT WAS A DARK AND STORMY NIGHT

nce upon a time, someday, you will say to yourself, "I'm going to write my historical novel," and this time you mean it. It isn't just a notion or a yearning anymore; you feel ready to start.

Start how? Start where?

The ways and places to start are infinite. Starting at the beginning is one way, but not the only way. Quite likely, you don't really even know yet where the beginning is.

But don't let that stop you.

By this time, inside your mind and heart is a story that has become so compelling you feel you must share it with everybody who reads. It might take you months, or even years, to get it written, but you know you have to do it. That means you must find a way to start.

THE SYNOPSIS

In order to sell your novel, you have to be able to tell the publisher or the agent what you're offering. That means you must do a synopsis, which is a condensed presentation and summary of your great story.

Writing a practice synopsis before you've started your manuscript is a good way to indicate to yourself where your novel will begin and end, and what it will say. It forces you to organize your story and give it form. It makes you decide who your protagonist will be and whose point of view you'll use to tell the story.

The decisions you make in writing this practice synopsis might be way off from what you eventually choose for your book, of course. Storytelling has a force of its own, and that force might escape from the original form set out in your synopsis. If that happens, it means you've actually started revising already. Revision isn't just something you do after you've finished your manuscript; it's a constant process.

The synopsis is an early milestone on the journey of your storytelling. And seeing an early nutshell form of your book on paper should get you fired enough to start writing the novel.

IT WAS A DARK AND STORMY NIGHT...

Some writers don't feel they've really begun until they've composed a terrific first sentence.

Or maybe even a great opening paragraph that will grab and hold the reader's attention. Or until they've finished a really vivid first scene. So putting the initial written words of the novel on paper constitutes still another important milestone. That first sentence, paragraph, or scene may not survive, of course, but it gives momentum. If the beginning is good enough, it will survive as your beginning. Or, it might survive to stand somewhere else in the story, if a better opening turns up. On the other hand, it might just get wiped out as the story makes its way and your judgment improves. Or maybe as you continue the process of research, you might find that the whole premise of your opening is not valid, and you'll have to discard it. Don't let that discourage you. It means that you're getting smarter, and your story is getting truer.

DO I KNOW ENOUGH TO START?

Some writers don't believe they're ready to begin writing the story until they've finished all the research they can think of to do—until they're sure of everything. That's a logical approach, of course. The more factual knowledge, the less likelihood you'll have to throw out a lot of glorious prose when you find out that something you assumed to be true wasn't.

But one problem with delaying your start until the research is all done is that the research is never all done. You might think you've got all the facts you need, but in writing your very first paragraph you might realize suddenly that what you've said raises other questions. Maybe your protagonist starts to say something, but you're not sure what idioms or figures of speech they used at that time, or in his part of the country. Or he starts to do something with a tool or a farming implement, but you're not sure such a thing had been invented yet. Maybe your heroine goes out looking for a medicinal plant because her baby's sick, but you're not sure that plant even grows in the region where she lives. So then you'll have to do more research to satisfy yourself that what you've written has truth, or, at least, verisimilitude.

In other words, if you don't start writing until you're sure of absolutely everything, you might just never get started with the writing.

GETTING TO KNOW YOU

Another good way to get started is by creating a full and comprehensive biography of your protagonist, and then the biographies of all your main characters. If they are real historical figures, you will research everything you can find out about them: their looks, their health, their upbringing, their beliefs, their personalities, their idiosyncrasies, their dialects, their manners and mannerisms, everything they ever wrote or had written about them. There are inconsistencies in all persons, but mostly they are more or less true to themselves, and you can establish for yourself a character study that shows why and how they did the things they did, why they met or didn't meet their goals. Once you feel you know your character totally, you will have reached another sort of milestone. You will be able to set that character in motion, because you'll know how he's motivated and how he operates. You will know how he speaks, how he carries himself. You will know his biography so well, you can refer to it in your head as readily as on paper.

You will be amazed at some of the things you decide to include in that biography. The closer you come to being your fictional character, the more intimately you'll want to know him, or her.

Writing a practice synopsis before you've started your manuscript is a good way to indicate to yourself where your novel will begin and end, and what it will say. It forces you to organize your story and give it form.

One of my favorite memories stems from an exhilarating night back in the mid-1980s, when actor Hal Holbrook came to Indiana University to do his Mark Twain portrayal onstage. A friend and reader of mine who was a Holbrook fan thought it would be enlightening if an actor and a novelist compared notes on the ways they research the historical personages they present.

So an arrangement was made to keep a Bloomington restaurant and bar open late, and we went there for dinner and refreshments after Mr. Holbrook's evening performance. It was a really good idea. Mr. Holbrook is a pleasant, intelligent, patient man who can hold his liquor and talk coherently all night long and, even better, listen with sincere interest to others. He told about certain research challenges he faced in preparing to "be" Mark Twain or Abraham Lincoln. For example, he needed to know, what did President Lincoln's voice sound like? No phonograph had existed in his lifetime to record it. What did he look like when he smiled or grinned? The photography of his day required long, posed exposures, and how long can someone hold the pose of showing his teeth and saying "cheese?" Therefore, Lincoln's photographic portraits, though numerous, show him grave or deadpan. But he was known to be a genuine humorist and jokester. How could an actor portray such a man onstage without knowing those things?

So Mr. Holbrook told of the time and effort he spent looking up in old newspapers and memoirs the impressions of people who had encountered Abraham Lincoln. He learned that his voice was rather high-pitched and ringing, sometimes almost bugle-like, which must have been an asset for an outdoor orator amid big crowds in those days before microphones and amplifiers. And Holbrook was pleased to find, here and there, descriptions of Lincoln's dazzling smile, his straight, white teeth—a rarity for a mature man in those days of primitive oral hygiene. As for Mark Twain, Holbrook found that the celebrated literary giant was quite small in stature. That discovery led Holbrook to have oversized furniture made to carry on his Twain tours, and even to order extra-big cigars for Twain to puff on and gesticulate with during his soliloquies, so that all would be to scale.

Of course, an actor who impersonates historic figures needs to research that way, because he has to make them visually and audibly real for his audience.

But so must a novelist, because, don't ever forget, the reader of the novel is likewise going to see and hear the character, as intimately as is an audience in a theater with Hal Holbrook. Maybe even more so, as the reader might find himself occupying a drafty, smoky room with the character, or watching the character wrestle with his conscience, or seduce or be seduced. The reader might even become the character.

I told Mr. Holbrook about such things as "phantom limb" syndrome, by which an amputee like George Rogers Clark still feels the sensations of his missing foot and leg. I told him about the bed in old General Clark's room at Locust Grove in Kentucky; the bed was stacked with cushions because the fluid in his lungs made it necessary for him to sleep sitting up—a result of all those cold, wet days and nights spent soldiering on the frontier. And I told him of the rheumatism pains stemming from those same ordeals. And, following all that, I told Holbrook about the research the novelist must do to learn what remedies Clark probably took for his ailments—the main ones being rum or whiskey.

By the time Mr. Holbrook and I finished comparing notes on character research, the sun was rising and customers were coming in for breakfast. Mr. Holbrook had a plane to catch.

There is much to be learned and done in researching character. You the historical novelist might not have all that intimate knowledge of your character written down in his biographical sketch before you start writing. But as you become your character, you will realize that you need to know at least as much as an actor needs to know. Author and actor are doing the same thing: bringing someone to life. And bringing truth to life.

GOOD YUCKY STUFF

When things go wrong, somebody always says, "Well, surely some good will come of it."

Throughout history, and long before written history, some of the best things in life have appeared as results of something gone wrong.

Take wine, beer, and whiskey, for example. Unless you're a teetotaler, you're glad they exist. But long ago, some mishap occurred—some overripe grapes began to ferment, some grain meal got wet in storage and started smelling sourish—and humans, just by accident, discovered that microorganisms, such as yeast cells, might be among man's best friends. Of course, ages went by before the microscope was invented and all those tiny fermenting creatures could be seen, but by then brewers and distillers were already making libations so exquisite that connoisseurs had arisen to judge their excellence. Yeast also accidentally brought man to the wondrous art of breadmaking and baking, as did the sourdough that was created when other kinds of food went bad.

Much the same thing happened when milk soured and clabbered, and before man really understood the process, we were enjoying piquant and delicious varieties of cheese and yogurt. Some of the processes were caused by rennin, an enzyme from calf stomachs, which sounds yucky, but was also collected and used to make lovely, soft dishes called junkets. Few people are still alive who remember eating junket. But some of the people in your historical novel probably enjoyed it.

Fermentation and other forms of natural spoilage have benefited us with composted fertilizer, sewage treatment, medicines, and many other blessings now under the heading of microbiology, including the discoveries of scientists like Louis Pasteur, who learned to keep them under control.

These quiet accidents and discoveries have had more important impact on us than even war and commerce, and are dramatic background for the human narrative, but few historical novelists ever give them a thought. Learn about such things, and keep them in mind.

Whether you ever write about them or not, you need to know of them, or you'll be missing one of the greatest underlying currents in the River of History.

LOOK WHO'S TALKING

You might decide to tell your story not through the eyes of your real historical figure, but instead through some real or imaginary character who is always nearby and involved. That's something a novelist can do that a historian can't.

There exist several good reasons to use a fictional character as the point-of-view person in a well-researched novel about real people and events. Your fictional character might bring a particular attitude or skepticism into a story that needs it for balance. Or that character might be a hero-worshiper whose adulation will illuminate the main hero, or, on the other hand, be dashed by the hero's failings.

A made-up character might also be there as the vehicle for a subplot. As I've said, it's hard for a historical novelist, restrained by the facts of known history, to do any plotting. But the made-up character can be engaged in some relevant personal conflict in the midst of the actual events, and that sub-plot might broaden the reader's understanding of the historical event. In my wife's novel about Nonhelema, the great Shawnee woman chief, she wrote about the soul and feelings of the chief from the point of view of that woman. I took the liberty of creating a cowardly frontier militiaman who admires Nonhelema and is so inspired by her courage that he surmounts his cowardice and becomes a braver and better man—even, eventually, her biographer. This fictional character, Dr. Case, provides gender balance, a white viewpoint, a new dimension to the novel, and also serves as an example of those important but unsung frontier scriveners whose old papers and memoirs have survived to be the sources of much of our research: men such as Dr. Lyman Draper, whose collected papers at the University of Wisconsin are the mother lode for research on the Old Northwest Territory. Although my fictional Dr. Case is eyewitness to many of her dramatic scenes in the book, he doesn't do anything that alters the real events.

He was a made-up character. But I was pleased to learn that some readers found him so real that they tried to Google him and find out more about him.

In another novel about real men and events, I needed to show the book's central character—a notorious deserter from the U.S. Army in the Mexican-American War—not through his own eyes, but through the eyes of the Americans he deserted and the Mexicans he joined. So I invented a fictional character for each side of the conflict. And I made both of them boys: an Irish-American

Army camp errand boy and a Mexican student cadet. Through their involvement with the main character on both sides of the border, their lives eventually intertwine. I used boys instead of adult soldiers for the respective viewpoints because children see war in a different way from adult soldiers, and also because children are war's especial victims.

Boy soldiers might also help younger readers to get absorbed enough in their stories to learn something about a war—which created most of our present-day immigration problems on the border with Mexico—that's scarcely mentioned in American History classes. A young reader might be drawn into a story of history by identifying with a young narrator, and, then, just by chance, learn some real history when it is timely to know it. Those are some of the uses of fictional characters in historical novels. They might help you start your story, and they probably will make it more human.

WHAT, AND HOW BIG?

You have two big things you need to work out in order to start writing your novel:

First, the gist of the story.

Second, the scope of the story.

As I said before, you might need a synopsis in order to sell your idea to a publisher. Even before then, making that synopsis will help you determine the gist and the scope of your novel. But it won't do the whole job for you.

The gist of the story is, of course, its heart and its significance. It is what makes you feel that you must tell the story. You might call it the "foregone conclusion." But that doesn't mean it won't change as you go along, learning as you go.

To write your synopsis, you'll need a sense of the scope of the story. Scope can mean "from when to when," but it should mean more than that. The scope also gives the sense of the consequences of whatever happens in your narrative: historical consequences, as in land, wealth, ideals, or power gained or lost. Or psychological consequences, as in the growth or diminution of your protagonist, his family and his dreams. Remember this: A great story means more than it says. However grand your narrative, the reader should understand something beyond the particulars of the tale you've told.

You might or might not have a real sense of that scope when you begin writing the story, but you'll have enough to get you started. If that hasn't grown wider and deeper by the end of your tale, you might not have told it well enough.

But you won't know that until you get there. First, you have to start: "Once upon a time it was now...."

A story's beginning place is sometimes chosen by intuition. Often that intuition is as good as rational plotting. A good storyteller likely has a natural starting sense and a quitting sense. Good starting places are such as these:

- birth (of the protagonist)
- a sunrise
- coming of age
- first bully
- first love, sexual or platonic
- funeral (preceding flashbacks?)
- enlistment
- first combat
- adultery
- a sail on the horizon
- start of a journey
- a bugle call

- discovery of a lump: gold? cancer?
- throb of distant drums
- a scream in the dark
- a sentry hit by an arrow
- discovery of a footprint
- waking from an ominous dream
- approaching hoofbeats
- a bolt of lightning (as in, "it was a dark and stormy night...")

Such beginnings have this good quality in common: They are immediate, and full of portent. These are called "grabbers." No time is wasted easing the reader into the story, because few readers have the patience that novel readers used to have.

You might or might not have a real sense of that scope when you begin writing the story, but you'll have enough to get you started. If that hasn't grown wider and deeper by the end of your tale, you might not have told it well enough.

Not too long ago, novels were read not just for enjoyment, but to pass the time, to fill vacant hours. There was no television or e-mail to distract the attention, and a reader was happy to wallow through pages of prose that might do nothing but describe a setting — an estate, a parlor, a landscape. Starting slow, getting to know the family, the society, the surroundings: that was the reader's pleasure in those halcyon times, before both parents had to work two jobs each to keep the car's gas tank filled. Just as political and economic understanding has been reduced to bumper stickers and sound bytes, and "attention deficit disorder" has become a plague, the patience of readers has shortened.

Readers are being made impatient by the increased tempo of life and the vast choice of storytelling vehicles competing for attention. When every action movie starts with an explosion or an orgasm, every TV drama with a suicide, kidnapping, or the discovery of a pole-dancer's mutilated corpse, readers get out of the habit of mood-building or scene-setting prose and want to cut to the chase. And so we have the "grabber" opening, even in a big, complex novel. If the reader isn't hooked in the first paragraph, the book likely won't get read—or even bought.

A good writer can, of course, instantly snag the reader not just by a startling action—like a scream in the dark or a bolt of lightning—but by language itself. George Orwell's *1984* begins: "It was a bright cold day in April, and the clocks were striking thirteen." What reader can ignore a beginning like that?

Or Norman Maclean's opening sentence in *A River Runs Through It:* "In our family, there was no clear line between religion and fly fishing."

There are many lessons in a good example. Consider my favorite beginning and ending of a novel to show how well it can be done. Ernest Hemingway's *For Whom the Bell Tolls* wasn't a historical novel when he wrote it, but that was so many wars ago that it is now.

It begins like this: "He lay flat on the brown, pine-needled floor of the forest, his chin on his folded arms, and high overhead the wind blew in the tops of the pine trees."

It comes around to end like this: "He could feel his heart beating against the pine needle floor of the forest."

This is good, clear, evocative writing. But the reason it is such a magnificent example of beginning and ending is that the "he" who lies prone on pine needles, Robert Jordan, is an intelligent and courageous idealist with a dangerous mission to do in a short few days in the midst of another country's civil war. Between that beginning and that ending, the story touches on everything concerning life, love, and death.

In the beginning, he is lying on the pine needles with binoculars studying the mountain riverscape where he must dynamite a bridge to keep it from being used by the enemy before a major battle. He is relying on a band of Spanish guerrillas who hide in these mountains and fight against the Fascists. He is fighting for their country, but he is not a Spaniard, he's one of many American idealists who went there to fight Fascism because he believed it was everybody's enemy. The reader gradually learns all this as the adventure builds.

In the end, Robert Jordan is again lying on pine needles, his leg broken, knowing he is about to die. He has succeeded in detonating the bridge with the help of the brave guerillas, but some things have gone wrong, as they do in war, and now he has this final duty, which is to cover the flight of the guerrillas from the pursuing enemy cavalry. He is waiting for the cavalry to come within range of his submachine gun. He is watching for the cavalry officer to ride into the sunlight across the clearing. Robert Jordan knows that ambushing the cavalry troop is the last thing he will do in his life, and he is trying not to think of pain or anything else but his final duty; his heart is beating against the pine needles.

Hemingway had the wisdom to end it with heartbeats—not with blazing combat like a Rambo movie—because death was so inevitable it wasn't needed to finish the story. So much has happened that a reader might not even remember consciously how it started, but there will be the sense of completion. There are the pine needles.

That is the art of beginning and ending. I say that in tribute to a writer who was a master of beginning and ending stories. Including, tragically, his own life story.

Chapter Ten

AIN'T LIKE
IT USED TO WAS

rom the moment you start writing your historical novel, you'll be in a different world. You will have to feel that previous time as acutely as if you were living in it. You'll have to pretend that you don't know anything that has happened since then, or anything that has been invented since then.

To put your readers there and make them feel at home in that time, you must teach them what something is the moment they see it, and make it seem like they've known it all along.

Few modern-age people can remember, or even imagine, the discomforts of old-time clothing: rough wool chafing the skin, the clammy, clinging heaviness of wet deerskins, the torturous constriction of corsets and stays. And try to imagine breaking in a pair of stiff boots made identical: not a left or a right foot. The feel of clothing is a very immediate and personal experience. As for laundering it by hand, that was hard, miserable work, and was done as seldom as could be, so a part of the clothing experience was the smell of what you wore.

For example, something you've always taken for granted, something as commonplace as switching on the electric lights when entering a room, probably couldn't be done in the time of your story. So, you'll have to think with a figurative candle or oil lamp in your hand. And before the early nineteenth century, you wouldn't even have been able to strike a match to light that candle, or to light up a smoke, because matches hadn't been invented yet. You might need to keep in mind that in the time of your novel, the cigarette probably hadn't yet been invented. Before that, there were cigars, but before cigars, most tobacco was chewed, sniffed as snuff, or smoked in pipes. And in those days, smokers didn't have to go outdoors to light up, or even ask, "Do you mind if I smoke?"

If your novel is set in Europe before the discovery of America, there won't be any smokers at all. Tobacco originated in America.

You will have to imagine a world without engines and motors—without their ubiquitous noise, without their labor-saving convenience. You'll have to keep in mind that if you want to ride somewhere, you must saddle a horse or harness it to some sort of a carriage, and it will be a good idea to learn how to do that, so you can describe it.

If you want water to drink or wash in, you can't just reach over and turn on a faucet. You'll have to keep in mind that water has to be dipped up, or drawn by muscle power from a well or cistern, then carried. And if it's to be hot water, someone must build a fire to heat it.

The past was not just a different time, it was a different place. Back then, the time was now, and the place was here. That is, it was familiar. People looked around and saw things, and knew what they were. If someone from back then came to the present time and saw cars and computers, airplanes with contrails in the sky, tractors in the fields, skyscrapers in the cities, the neon glitter of a big town, or a TV set flickering its pictures in a living room, that visitor wouldn't know what it all was, wouldn't have names for any of it.

Likewise, when we go back to that other time, and take our readers back with us, we will see things we don't recognize and can't name. It will be a different place because it's so unfamiliar. Modern folks don't know what old things were, or what they were called.

That means that you, the writer of the historical novel, will have to put your readers down in the middle of that unfamiliar place called the past, in such a way that they won't feel alien or bewildered by strangeness. To put your readers there and make them feel at home in that time, you must teach them what something is the moment they see it, and make it seem like they've known it all along. It would be culture shock for someone from the twenty-first century to awaken back in a pre-Industrial Revolution landscape, if you, their author and guide, didn't instantly familiarize them with it. Tell them what things were called, show how things were used, and how things were done.

A good example is this from *Fearless,* Lucia St. Clair Robson's nitty-gritty novel about battlefield nurse and adventuress Sarah Bowman in the Mexican-American War. In it, Sarah goes to a famously lice-infested Mexican jail to question a prisoner:

"She had wrapped her ankles in vinegar-soaked rags to discourage the vermin from hopping aboard there, and she held her skirts up so that no lice or fleas could stow away in the hems."

Or, look at this flashback to a scene of childhood life on the Claffey plantation in Georgia, from MacKinlay Kantor's *Andersonville,* my favorite American historical novel.

> While Lucy was still very young the exploits of Florence Nightingale were discussed in newspapers and magazines. Lucy burned to emulate the Englishwoman, and was discovered to have set up a hospital in a bake house which had been damaged by a fire and was not being used at the time. She had five unwilling small blacks for patients and was dosing them with her father's best brandy and Trask's Magnetic Ointment which she had prepared out of lard, raisins and fine cut tobacco. Her brothers dubbed her Florence Nightmare and applied the name until she stormed into tears; then they were contrite.

The flashback shows a snippet of nineteenth-century childhood, with humor, but implicit sadness: As the novel progresses, those brothers of hers are being killed in distant Civil War battles. And the flashback is also prophetic. The adult Lucy will be called into nurse duty by the overworked prison doctor.

GUIDING THE READER

To envision the difference between early America and our country as it is today requires a vast, transformative leap of the imagination: This was an agricultural country, and no one in those days, even visionary thinkers like Thomas Jefferson, ever anticipated that it would be anything else. It looked different, and most human perceptions about it were different. You the historical novelist will have to prepare for that enormous shifting of gears. Most visible human activity was the herding and harvesting of food and the collection of fuel.

Likewise, the rest of the world was pre-Industrial Revolution, much of its economy and culture was subsistence farming, or hunting or herding, and even the cities depended on those productions. Most everything now made in corporate factories and mills was then produced at home or in town shops by journeymen and apprentices: clothing, tools, ironwork, weaponry, house wares, and utensils. And the population was incredibly sparse compared with the present days' burgeoning billions. It was a world that looked different, felt different, *was* different. As I mentioned before, a vague awareness of frontiers prevailed. Distances between places were daunting, because travel was so slow and difficult.

As much as you can, you must be like someone who has lived there, because you're going to be not just the storyteller but also the tour guide taking your readers through the past.

If you guide your reader down a road of the past, that road won't be pavement of any kind, but probably a hoofbeaten dirt trail with wagon-wheel ruts, or, in a more "advanced" state, a road of logs laid over the mud. Your reader must at once see and hear and feel and understand that, and expect to slog or push a wagon through the mud if it rains, or to breathe and blink against dust if it doesn't. Your reader must be familiar with the smells of horse or oxen manure in the road, the sounds of hoofbeats and footsteps and creaking harness and the commands of teamsters to their teams, the crack of a whip, the sound of horse farts. The reader you take with you on a road through the past must feel either uneven dirt underfoot or the saddle under his weary butt or the daylong, bone-shaking impact of a hardwood wagon seat, and think nothing of it because that's just what travel was like, back when "then was now."

Along the road, the reader may see a wide area of clear-cut woods with raw stumps standing, hear axes and saws, smell dense, acrid smoke, and see blackened mounds of earth shimmering with heat while soot-covered men work around them with long-handled rakes. At once, the reader must understand that he's passing a charcoal manufactory, something that was common then but forgotten now: a place where piles of wood were burned with limited air to make charcoal.

The reader must not think, in the twenty-first century way, "Gee, they must have had lots of patio cookouts to use that much charcoal," but instead understand that charcoal was the superhot fuel used in foundries and blacksmith shops. You must teach such things as you lead the reader through the story, because such things were common then, part of the economic works of the time. The blacksmith is a figure still vaguely remembered from the past, thanks to Longfellow's famous poem, "The Village Blacksmith," and chances are that a blacksmith will be needed to repair a weapon or shoe your hero's horse before your novel is done. So the reader ought to know where that charcoal in his forge comes from, as it was all a part of life in those days. The reader should also be able to see how the blacksmith works with his tools, where he gets his iron, what his apprentice does in the shop to help him shape a horseshoe or temper a steel blade. Many modern readers don't even know what an apprentice was.

Or a drover. Along the roads in the old days, men drove herds of cattle and sheep many miles to market, as they didn't have trucks or trains to carry them. The drovers lived outdoors the entire time they were on such moves, and they were really hardy folks. Herds on the move were a common sight.

Charcoal burners, blacksmiths, gunsmiths, coopers, teamsters, wheelwrights, wainwrights, liveries, tanners, innkeepers—those were all occupations along the road in the old days, and you, the author, cannot create that road through your story without researching them and making them vivid for the reader. To neglect that would be like describing a highway trip across the modern United States without showing a gas station, a motel, an auto parts store, a McDonald's at the off-ramp, a semi driver eating eggs and hash browns at a noisy truck stop, or the cop in his patrol car waiting behind the underpass to catch you speeding. If you don't know what those old occupations were, how they were done, and how they interacted with the passersby, you're not prepared to write a historical novel. A historical figure doesn't pass through a blank countryside. That means you, the novelist, must learn by research what the whole place was like in those times. As much as you can, you must be like someone who has lived there, because you're going to be not just the storyteller but also the tour guide taking your readers through the past.

Indeed, that's one of the reasons why many people like to read historical novels. They want to see and feel the road their forebears came by. They might have people named Cooper or Wright or Miner or Cook or Hunter or Archer in their family tree and know there was a time when people were named for what they did. They are citizens of a country, and they want to understand how the country came to be what it is. They know it wasn't always this easy or comfortable a place to live in, and they want to have a notion of what had to be done to make it this way. They will pick up your novel with the expectation of having a vivid sojourn through their own family or national or ethnic history. They want it to be an experience and an education—not just a tale.

UNDERCURRENTS

Besides just the things they can see along the road in your novel, the readers must understand other, unseen things that existed and were important then, and you must make them aware of those things.

For example, if your novel is set before 1864 in America, your reader will be in a country that allowed and even promoted slavery. That is no small detail; it would have been a powerful undercurrent in the conscious mind of every historical character you write about.

If your novel takes place on other continents, in even more ancient times, people other than Africans might be the slaves in your novel. There's no race that wasn't enslaved at one time or other. Some American Indians were sold into slavery by the Pilgrims. Aztecs in Mexico enslaved other tribes. Spaniards came and enslaved Aztecs. Some Cherokee Indians owned black slaves. Romans enslaved Celts and Nubians. Egypt enslaved Hebrews. At various times, the sorry fact is, just about anybody could enslave anybody else if they could catch them. Think of that great historical novel of Roman times, *Spartacus,* by Howard Fast. Those gladiators who rebelled were slaves, and they were of every race.

It's a rare historical novel that couldn't, realistically, contain slavery, or the underlying awareness of slavery, in it. And in addition to outright slavery, there were other ways of owning people and their labor. Many immigrants to America, perhaps even your own ancestors, came over in servitude as bondsmen or indentured servants, contracted to serve a year, or years, for someone who had paid their sea passage. Many men and their families who were presumed to have arrived as free persons actually didn't. That can complicate any tale of the past; it could even be a main theme of your historical novel. And there were other economic treadmills that so-called free men were running in place on—tenant farming, sharecropping, child labor, the "company store"—these are almost forgotten now, but prevailed then.

You, the author, must know also about the various kinds of laws—statutory and moral laws—that were in existence in the period you're writing about, because the characters in your novel will be abiding by those laws, or violating them. If you haven't researched those laws, you might well let a character in your story blithely get away with something that would have gotten him or her arrested or lynched or tarred and feathered, or simply castigated in the community. There have been times and places in world history, even American history, when churchmen had the authority to stride into the taverns and tell—not just suggest, but *tell*—any customer that he'd had enough.

You probably have never given it a thought, but until Dr. Samuel Johnson compiled his *Dictionary of the English Language* in 1755, there was no standard way to spell English words. If your protagonist is writing a letter, he will write it the way it sounds to him. And such phonetic spelling will depend on the dialect familiar to him, or to her.

As a writer, you should know what they used to write with in the time of your story. Were they still using pens made of quills then, or had the steel nib pen been invented? Might a lady have a glass pen? When were pencils available? People in your novel probably will write at least a time or two. You have to know how they did it and when, because you'll have to describe it. Learn to make a quill pen. Get to know inkwells, sealing wax, sand bottles, blotters. Try using them.

THE TIMES THEY WERE A-CHANGIN'

The time period in which your novel is set will be characterized by certain prevailing experiences and thoughts that will be in the minds of your characters, and you should know what they are before you even begin your storytelling. Depending on the chronological period, there will be climate extremes, droughts, times of famine, plagues, invasions, waves of superstition, periods of religious passion, and inquisitions. Just as we now face the effects of global warming, civilizations and their food supplies were profoundly affected by five centuries of uncommon cold, known as the "Little Ice Age," between the medieval times and the nineteenth century, sometimes exacerbated by sun-blocking atmospheric pollution from volcanic eruptions half a world away. Similarly, most of the horrendous "acts of God" in the Bible's Old Testament have been explained by the explosive eruption of a Mediterranean volcano, of which the island Santorini is believed to be the remainder. The same catastrophe is sometimes said to be the basis for the legend of Atlantis.

The time period in which your novel is set will be characterized by certain prevailing experiences and thoughts that will be in the minds of your characters, and you should know what they are before you even begin your storytelling.

The period of your novel might also be overshadowed by fears and hopes growing from religious events like the rise and fall of

Mohammedanism, the Crusades, the Reformation. And when you pick the time of your story, you must know what the populations believed about witchcraft and alchemy at that time. And had Marco Polo's revelations about Oriental splendor swept Europe yet?

And what was the state of commerce in the time of your story? The so-called "global economy" is nothing new. Traders of the Hanseatic League were sailing the known seas, and explorers were finding new ones. Cibola, the City of Gold, was being sought by conquistadors in the New World, and people expected that a fountain of youth would be found, to give them immortality.

As a novelist, you must, of course, consider what the state of literacy was in the time and place of your tale. Had Gutenberg's invention of moveable type yet brought books within reach? Substantial portions of the people in historic times didn't read or write. What were the bridges between the literate and the illiterate? At times there were whole subcultures of clerks, notaries, scribes, and amanuenses who did all the record-keeping and correspondence in certain civilizations.

I have written three novels in which the main protagonists were illiterate, which means that I, a literary man by trade, have had to imagine the condition of illiteracy, something I can't even remember. I could read before kindergarten. (When I was still too small to reach the dining table, my parents put a dictionary or an encyclopedia on a chair for me to sit on, and so I learned to read by a process I call "Assmosis." Feel free to believe or disbelieve that, as you choose.)

To make an illiterate protagonist "live" is a challenge. We who read and write exist in a different frame of mind from those who can't; we perceive differently, and we remember differently. We aren't necessarily *smarter* than illiterate people. I, with a houseful of books and a brain clogged with book learning, might well be outwitted by an aborigine whose natural mode of thinking could be far more clear and agile than mine. As a literate military officer with a map, I still might need a scout with his instinctual "feel" for the lay of the land. Polynesians with no written language or navigational charts could find their way from tiny island to tiny island in the vast Pacific using their knowledge of stars, currents, and clouds, and Australian Aborigines roamed their immense land without getting lost, by way of a sort of memorized "road song," which was like an undrawn map of their whole subcontinent. Not to dwell too much on the subject, but I do like to advise the would-be historical novelist to keep in mind that, through much of human history, most people were illiterate. An infinite variety of stories could be built just on that premise.

What could be more exciting and inspiring, for example, than a novel about, say, a slave learning to read and write? It's a topic touched upon in my wife's genealogy chapter earlier in this book.

Years ago, I met a black woman in Ohio whose last name was Ditto. Then I came across that odd name a few more times. Research showed me how it happened. On tax rolls, wills, and such documents, slaves often had given names only, such as John or Mary, and were listed as property, under the name of their owner. His name would be at the top of the ledger page, and on lines below, his slaves' names would be listed, as:

John ditto

Mary ditto

Moses ditto ...

Somewhere along the way in the keeping of records, then, Ditto became a surname. A poignant reminder of parts of our history that we'd rather forget ....

Hey, I just gave myself a good idea for a historical novel! But you're welcome to use it, if you can write it before I do.

CODES AND MORES

As the novelist who guides your reader through the milieu of a past time, you need to know—even before you write—about such archaic matters as codes of honor, such as dueling, for example. It's a shock to have to think of it, because it's been so thoroughly banished, but a gentleman needed to be careful what he said about another in the period between the sixteenth and the nineteenth centuries, when dueling was legal and even fashionable. Aside from Aaron Burr's killing of Alexander Hamilton, or Andrew Jackson's readiness to give and take honorable offense, American history often neglects the practice of the formal duel. But any man involved in public life in those times had to keep in mind that if he didn't control his tongue, he might face the sword or pistol of an offended gent on some foggy morning. Newspaper editors were often

---

COSTUME PORN

The stereotypical so-called "bodice-ripping" historical novels that gave our genre its raffish reputation were often escapist fantasies. The heaving bosoms, the passion percolating beneath bustles and hoop skirts, were created to titillate readers. I call much of that stuff "costume porn."

But it's not anachronistic to write erotica into good historical fiction. Lust and sexual virtuosity weren't invented in the twentieth century. Men and women, boys and girls (and men and boys, too), have been rutting and coupling forever. Even when contemplating the idyllic tragedy of Romeo and Juliet, remember that randy teenagers have always been randy teenagers.

My long-time editor Pamela Strickler once startled me by commenting on the first draft of my novel *Follow the River*: "It needs some sex." Sex? In a wilderness survival novel consisting mainly of solitude, starvation, and extreme hardship? Besides that, sex was just what a descendant of the heroine had begged me *not* to put in when she learned I was writing about her ancestor. She was a proper old Christian lady who feared my historical novel would be a bodice-ripper, and I had assured her that wasn't my intent. In fact, there was no place for sex scenes in that true story at all. So the sexiness had to occur in the memories, yearnings, and imaginations of the heroine and her distant husband. (The husband's fantasies became so vivid that the novel was banned from one Indiana high school recommended-reading list on the complaints of a student's mom, who thought they would give her son "impure thoughts.")

If your (high-class) historical novel has sex scenes, though, don't write them from the modern mindset. Sexual coupling in any time is basically the same act, but society — and the copulators themselves—had different attitudes at different times (and very little Sex Ed as we know it), and the old, lewd vocabularies show that prim Victorianism was really quite an aberration. Men wore codpieces to attract notice; women didn't wear underpants in the olden times. When did they start?

Was the douche bag or the condom invented yet at the time of your story? Who had been circumcised and who hadn't? Were the venereal diseases transatlantic by then? Was the "f" word in use by then? (Was it really an acronym from the words FOR UNLAWFUL CARNAL KNOWL-EDGE graven on the pillory where fornicators were locked up?) Do you know what a french letter is, and would it have been in use at the time of your story?

You have to know. That means research. Probably the world's most complete and best-organized collection of sexual data is the Kinsey Institute at Indiana University, which happens to be half an hour's drive from where I live. I haven't been there myself. But if I start writing more sex scenes in my historical novels, that's where I'll go for research on old-timey sex. I recommend, go and do thou likewise, before you start ripping bodices.

called to the "field of honor" for writing such editorials as we see every week in the modern newspaper. (If dueling over editorial remarks were legal today, Dick Cheney might have shot at me several times a year). The outspoken Mark Twain in his newspapering days once practiced for a duel by trying in vain to hit a barn door with pistol shots. And Abraham Lincoln once admitted that the two things he really rued in his life as a state legislator were "jumping out of the Statehouse window to avoid a quorum," and letting himself get involved in a duel. (The duel was not quite consummated, fortunately. Being the challenged party, Lincoln cleverly chose sabers wielded from behind marked lines, and when the challenger saw the advantage given by Lincoln's long arm, he allowed himself to be talked out of it.)

The point I'm making is that many things were different in the past, both in the obvious physical world and in the customs and laws of those times, things virtually forgotten now but so important back then that you, the historical novelist, can't write truly about those times without doing deep, wide research on topics you never imagined you'd need to know. As I've said before in this book, you have to create in words the whole world through which your story progresses.

WITHIN YOUR SKIN

Your readers will have to adapt not just to the past they're passing through, but to the past that's passing through them.

What I mean by that weird statement is that modern readers will have to forget what they know about germs and viruses, vaccines and serums, hormones and pheromones, as well as all that stuff Freud came up with about ego, id, and superego. Until Darwin, you wouldn't have wondered about having simian ancestors. And forget IQ; there was no such thing until the twentieth century.

It takes real mental adjustment to imagine never having such things in your head.

During much of the time you'll write about, the temperaments, personalities, and even the intelligence of persons were believed to be governed by the proportions of the four "humours," or fluids, within their skins. Those humours were called sanguine, phlegmatic, choleric, and melancholy.

A man's nature was described according to the characteristics believed to result from whichever humour was dominant in him. A "choleric" character was hot-tempered, and probably shrewd and vengeful, because the humour "yellow bile" predominated. In my own early lifetime, persons of that sort were called "bilious." Some old folks still use that adjective.

A melancholy person was then, as now, abnormally sad and even depressed, and in those days it was attributed to an excess of the humour known as "black bile." Black bile gave you the blues. Remember that one of the most pathetic heroes in Western literature, Cervantes's Don Quixote de la Mancha, was known as "The Knight of the Sorrowful Countenance."

A "phlegmatic" person was impassive, insensitive, apathetic, because the humour phlegm was thought to be cold and moist and to cause sluggishness. Nowadays, of course, we think of phlegm mainly as mucus, of which snot is a particular sort, so we have "snotty" as a strong and ugly adjective for describing certain kinds of phlegmatic persons.

Blood was thought to be the dominant humour of a "sanguine" person, who looked and acted sturdy, ruddy, and cheerful. But if he edged over into "sanguinary," he might be likely to "see red" and try to shed someone else's blood, as Don Quixote himself did when some real or imaginary challenge got his blood pressure up.

The best sort of person was thought to be the one who had those four fluids, or humours, in balanced proportions. That one was called a good-humored person. It doesn't mean he had a good sense of humor, like a standup comedian, but that he had a good nature. Illnesses were thought to be results of humour imbalances, because no one suspected there were such things as germs and viruses.

My reason for giving all this background about the humours is that they were the basis on which people evaluated, explained, and described others and themselves in the days before psychology came into being as the science of mind and behavior. Your characters, throughout many of the centuries you'll be writing about, believed these humours were at work in all human nature. Therefore the theory will flavor their whole conscious life.

In literature, the influence of the humours had a heyday in the plays of Ben Jonson and William Shakespeare. In Act II, Scene I, of *Much Ado About Nothing*, Beatrice is described: "There's little of the melancholy element in her ... she had often dreamed of unhappiness and waked herself with laughing."

In other times and cultures, consciousness and behavior were thought to be controlled not by humours, but by demons and angels, or by Satan, by the inner struggle known as hadji, or by the ethos and philosophies of myriad religions. Wherever you go for your novel's story, you will find at least one of these undercurrents, and you will have to make your readers feel it.

You will not stop in the middle of your tale and write a dissertation on it, of course (by God, you'd better not!), but if you intend for your reader to understand your characters and their relation to each other, you must create the sense of such influences in their times. If you don't, you'll have modern human beings peopling the past, and that's the sin of anachronism.

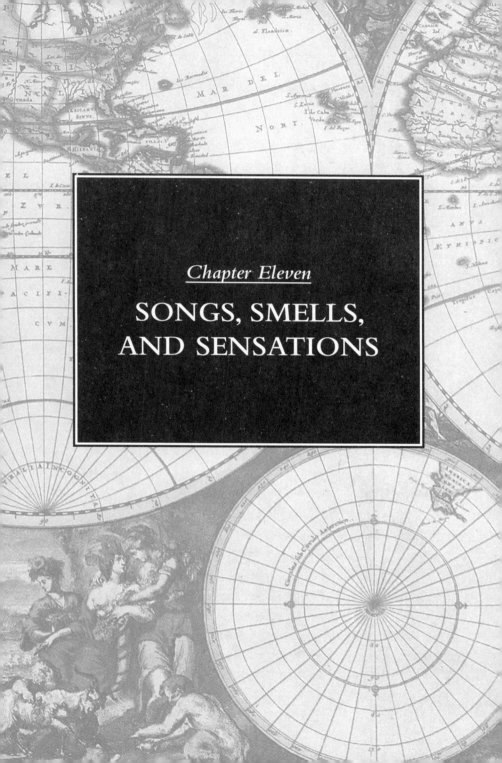

Chapter Eleven

SONGS, SMELLS, AND SENSATIONS

suspect that one reason young people don't like reading history very much is that they grew up with movies and television, which always are filled end to end with noise: musical scores, canned laughter, gunfire, sirens, thumps, crashes, groans, and screams.

A book, on the other hand, is silent.

Life, especially the dramatic and evocative parts of life throughout history, is full of noise: Drums, bugles, bagpipes, and war cries resound through the history of war, along with the clanging of steel against steel weapons and the horrible sounds of weapons smashing skulls and rending flesh.

In peacetime, there was always music, and before it was recorded by Mr. Edison's phonograph, most people made their own music. Some scientists believe that primitive human beings sang wordless songs before they had verbal language. Laborers often sang to keep cadence in their work, women to soothe their children or to reinforce their own hopes and dreams.

But a book is silent.

Or is it?

It shouldn't be.

MAKING YOUR BOOK HEARD

I mentioned my old Butler University creative writing professor Dr. Beyer, who said, "Write to their senses." That meant the sense of hearing, as well as the others.

The actual sound of writing, in my long life at it, has been the scratch of pen and pencil on paper, or the clacking of old typewriters. This is the first book I've ever composed on a computer, and it's so quiet, it spooks me. But what I hear when I'm writing is not the pen or the typewriter or the PC's hum: It is the sound of whatever I would hear if I were in the scene I'm writing.

I want the reader to hear all that, too.

In all societies, music and dance have been important in the daily lives of the people. Even though a book is a silent object—words printed on pages—when the reader begins reading, as many senses are awakened as the author wants to evoke. The author should want to evoke all of them. And the sense of hearing is supremely important.

Songs written on paper look like poems. They tell something about the character and the preoccupations of the people back then who sang them. When people sing their familiar songs, in times of jubilation, or homesickness, or worship, or mourning, the songs become part of the story, of the particular scene. The reader should be able to "hear" the songs. A reader doesn't have to hear through ears. A nostalgic ballad can go directly from the printed page to the reader's brain, where the reader can hear it, along with the lyre or drums or guitars that accompany it, and thence to the heart.

Therefore, it is important to a good historical novelist to research the music of the past and learn it well enough to convey it right into the reader's conscious. Sound is always part of the ambience in real life, and music is one of the most meaningful of human sounds. Even if it's just a plaintive fragment of a love song or a few chords of fiddle music heard through a doorway by a lonely passerby, it can make a written scene memorable, just as does, say, a distant train whistle.

Or the evocative author can, by intelligent choice of the song, even reveal or enhance the gist of the scene or bring back a powerful memory or plant an omen pertaining to a later scene.

Toward the end of *Sign-Talker,* my novel about the French-Shawnee frontiersman George Drouillard, I wanted to give a foreboding of his violent death. So, in a night camp beside the Missouri River, on a trapping expedition heading into Indian country, he hears boatmen at another campfire singing a very familiar old French children's melody:

> *Alouette, Gentille alouette,*
> *Alouette, je te plumerai!*
> *Je te plumerai la tete …*

Skylark, lovely skylark, Drouillard thought, remembering the song from the Black Robe school. Skylark, I am going to pluck your head. He shuddered.

Even though a book is a silent object—words printed on pages—when the reader begins reading, as many senses are awakened as the author wants to evoke.

Describing any sound well enough to make the reader "hear" it from a silent page is a challenge, and skillful use of adjectives is a good tool. Since almost every reader has heard a fiddle, you can simply say, as you describe a scene, that "faint fiddle music was coming from inside the house," and the reader will hear a fiddle in the mind's ear. But what kind of fiddle music would it be, in that time and place? Fast and lively, like a reel? Mournful? Melodic and sweet, as in a love song? Or harsh and angry like a tomcat's yowl? Who's playing it, and what's the player's mood?

What about drums? The rattle of a trap drum on the battlefield and the deep throb of a native drum in the jungle can both be ominous, but they sound unlike each other, and careful selection of adjectives can make the reader hear them as you intend them to be heard.

Singing voices are even more evocative and varied than musical instruments. If you write simply, "A woman was singing down in the valley," you're missing an opportunity to create a rich and meaningful sound effect for your reader. Singing what, and how? A ballad? A lullaby? A hymn? Something bawdy? Is her voice clear and sweet, or deep and sad? Are her words audible? Do they strike a chord with the mood of the protagonist, who is most likely the hearer? Is the voice reminiscent of some loved one? Is it muffled by fog or broken up by wind gusts into mere snatches of sound?

To practice "hearing" for your reader, listen to the sounds around you, wherever you are, and think of the words or phrases you could use to describe those sounds. Don't use a cliché; coin your own phrase, make your own original simile. Learn to listen to sounds not just as ambient noise, but as sounds that can be clearly described in words. A girl's laughter could be described as a sound like silver bells, but that's been done so often it's hackneyed. Same with an evil-tempered woman who "scolds like a magpie." That, too, is a cliché, and, furthermore, it would be of little help to a modern, urban reader who wouldn't know a magpie from a Cornish hen. (I once was provoked to tell a scold, "Ma'am, if I want to hear that tone of voice, I'll go run my chainsaw." It was a fitting comparison, but not one useful in historical fiction, of course, because chainsaws hadn't been invented yet in the old days of which I write.)

I remember as a student reading an evocative description by Ernest Hemingway, who said that a particular artillery shell flying over him sounded like canvas being ripped above his head. A few years later I had opportunity to confirm that with my own ears. I remembered at that moment his description and thought how accurate it was. From that I learned a good writing lesson about the making of similes: Keep them original and keep them accurate. The sounds of bombardment vary greatly, depending on what the ammunition is, and where you are when you hear it. If you're lucky enough never to have to hear it yourself, ask people who have, or research it in the archives of combat. It's too easy to say "the shell screaming over, punctuated with an earth-shaking blast." That's already been written thousands of times. And while you're describing such hellishness, be sure to describe its effect on the person in the midst of it. Most soldiers in combat areas have loose stools anyway (part of the "glory of war"), and it can get scared out of you by such sounds as ripping canvas in the sky. If your character in a story is in that kind of misery, you want to make your reader clench and squirm for him.

COWBELLS AND INDIANS

In 1792, an American army force under command of General Arthur St. Clair was nearly wiped out by an early morning Indian attack. In my research of that battle I learned that people who heard the attack from a couple of miles away likened the gunfire and cannonfire, not very surprisingly, to a thunderstorm. More surprising was a description of the distant war whoops as a sound like "ten thousand cowbells." You have to think on that a moment before it makes sense. But a distant war whoop does indeed ring like a bell.

Running onto an evocative phrase like that, perceived by someone's impressionable ear two centuries ago, makes a writer's day. Few modern readers have ever heard Indian war whoops, and probably never will, except maybe in a movie. (Few modern readers, for that matter, have ever heard a cowbell.)

That cowbell description was brought to my attention long ago by a scholar who has helped and guided me with my battle researches so many times that I would be an ingrate if I didn't acknowledge him here. I mean Martin West, longtime director of the Fort Ligonier Museum in Southwest Pennsylvania. Like countless authors, re-enactors and film researchers, I've not just stood on Marty's shoulders, but virtually marched on them.

An old American Indian friend of mine showed me how to make a whistle out of an eagle's wing bone. Then he put it to his lips and said, "Tell me if you recognize this sound," and blew through it. It sounded like one thing, and one thing only: the long, shrill, declining cry of an eagle soaring in the sky. In a later novel, I wrote of an Indian boy and a white man exchanging just such a gift, and the sound of that whistle being blown across the Missouri River as they parted. That was a most touching sound effect for a scene in a novel, and readers have told me that the scene brings tears to their eyes, because they could hear that bone-channeled eagle's cry, even though they were just reading silent ink-words on a book page about two friends who would never see each other again.

Another authentic (and useful) sound effect you could make heard in a historical novel is the town crier—that loud-voiced official who used to walk the streets of a town, ringing a bell, and announcing all the news that the townspeople needed and wanted to know. He was the evening newscast before there was radio or TV. The town crier can be a sound effect, and more, too, as his news itself might become a key part of your story.

So there is the power of sound told in writing, done, as my old writing teacher Werner Beyer used to insist, by "writing to their senses."

WHIFF-SNIFFING

Keep your own senses open, your antennae out. It works in all the senses.

The sense of smell is said by scientists to be the most evocative memory prompter. Your mood can be changed, for better or worse, by a whiff of something you haven't smelled since childhood, like, say, your father's shaving soap, or some dish you haven't smelled cooking since your grandmother made it half a century ago, or old substances like mothballs or camphor, or linseed oil in an artist's studio, or the first time you were close enough to smell the perfume behind a girl's ear. Memory by scent is useful, even though your printed page is odorless.

I say, practice it. A few years ago as my wife and I were on a suburban road in Ohio one mild night, we caught a faint and familiar scent in the slipstream by the car window. "Smell that?" she asked.

"I do," I said.

"Skunk or Starbucks?"

Of course, it doesn't take long to realize which, but the surprising thing is that for a moment, until it gets bad enough that you know it's skunk, it could be that dense and inviting aroma of dark-roast coffee.

I'm not trying to insult the coffee-shop chain when I urge you to pay attention the next time you get a slight whiff of one or the other. It doesn't seem a likely comparison. But most people I mention it to come back eventually and say, "You're right!"

What that has to do with writing is that writer and reader share the same senses, and you can be a better writer if you stay keenly conscious of scents and sounds, flavors and textures, and the ways of seeing things—use all the evocative power of our rich language to put your reader in the sensuous center of whatever scene you're writing.

And keep in mind that the past was quite smelly, back in those days before mouthwash and deodorants and flush toilets, before meat refrigeration; when towns had tanneries and stockyards and butcher shops; when public buildings had spittoons; when horse and ox manure paved the streets. To describe a stroll through a populated place in the "good old days," in a way that puts your reader right down in it, you could use half the adjectives in your vocabulary, especially the odorous ones.

On the other hand (while we're on the subject of animal poop), my personal field research up on the Great Plains surprised me in a pleasant way. Out there where there's hardly any firewood, the fuel for campfires and cookfires often was buffalo chips or cow chips: sun-dried dung. I gathered enough for an evening campfire on the bank of the Missouri and kindled it. I had never heard or read anything to prepare me for the smell of such a fire, so I stayed upwind at first. But that wasn't necessary because burning buffalo poop smells like burning grass. And why wouldn't it? Grass is what they eat.

....

And keep in mind that the past was quite smelly, back in those days before mouthwash and deodorants and flush toilets, before meat refrigeration; when towns had tanneries and stockyards and butcher shops; when public buildings had spittoons; when horse and ox manure paved the streets.

....

Next time you're cooking with buffalo poop (as you surely will), notice that it burns clean and almost smokeless. That is, if it's dry. Don't use it if it isn't. (You're welcome for that useful advice.)

In modern times, we don't use our sense of smell as much as man has done through the ages. Much has been done to suppress the stink of life. Our sense of smell has been damaged by chemical pollutants in the air. I live in a hardwood forest. The foliage constantly purifies the air here, and if a car goes by on the road a few yards away, I can smell its exhaust for several minutes afterward. Driving through a city is an assault on my sense of smell, because I'm not used to the chemicals, the industrial pollutants, or all that vehicular exhaust.

POTTY TALK

The novelist has the power to write a whole life story without ever sending his protagonist to the potty. Earlier generations of writers seldom dealt with that essential biological function.

But writers aren't as fastidious or demure as they used to be, and there are times when the characters in a book do get caught with their pants down. In my Mexican War novel, for example, a part of one key scene has the protagonist and a mortar shell arriving simultaneously at the latrine.

And in MacKinlay Kantor's great novel about the squalid Confederate prison camp at Andersonville, Georgia, the vast, open latrine is a major cause of the illnesses that killed thousands of the Yankee prisoners. That magnificent novel is literally knee deep in diarrhea.

I strongly advise you as a historical novelist to research the customs and technologies of waste disposal through the ages, as well as the myriad euphemisms and slang terms used at respective times. You can step into some nasty anachronisms if you don't watch out.

Don't have people excusing themselves to "go to the bathroom" if your story antedates indoor plumbing. Know how and when British folks used the terms "loo" and "W.C." Learn about chamberpots, and the "jakes," and look up the Chic Sale Special. Get the poop on why Muslims carry water containers to the john with them. Learn why the phrase "s--- on a stick" might have its origins in Ancient Rome. Research just when toilet paper arrived on the scene. What is the predominant smell Korean War veterans remember, and why?

As I've suggested elsewhere, know all you can learn about something even if you can't bring yourself to write about it.

(And, no, historic Waterloo wasn't the first flush toilet, as a student once guessed in an exam.)

Not so very long ago, people relied on their noses to find food and to avoid danger. Natural air was clean, and they could detect life scents in it. A bear smells like a barn. A rattlesnake smells like cucumbers. Man's sense of smell is much inferior to that of dogs and most other animals, and, of course, that's one reason why dogs are so useful to us in sniffing out game or danger or missing children or fugitives, and, in the modern world, drugs and explosives. I say elsewhere in this book that animals, both wild and domestic, will probably be very important somewhere in your historical novel. You can hardly write a historical story of any verisimilitude without animals. A part of research in daily life, when you don't even consciously think you're researching, is the close and caring observation of animal behavior.

I had an Irish setter long ago who liked to sit beside me under a big oak tree on the ridge here at sunset time. I was watching the sun go down over the valley, and my eyeballs moved. His nose was always quivering. He was smelling the wind to determine where it had been. I'm sure he was getting more information through his nose than I was through my eyes.

All the beasts, including humans, live and act according to the sensory stimuli they get. This was even more true in the old days, before we tamed the environment around us with deodorants and air fresheners, central heating and air conditioning, insulated clothing, and all the comforts and other stimulus-numbing innovations of modern life. Keep that in mind when you're researching and writing about the past. You want your reader to "be there" in the noisome past, so give them all the stenches, dins, eyesores, putridity, and physical discomforts that people dealt with in those days. And now and then write in a song, for your reader's ears.

SOME SENSORY EXERCISES

Now and then, practice writing strictly to the senses.

Here are a few exercises I've assigned to students in writing workshops:

1. Get a kumquat, persimmon, or some other fruit or vegetable you've never eaten before. Open it with your fingers, examine it, smell it, eat it slowly, close your eyes, lick, and chew, concentrating on everything you're doing and experiencing. Then write a thousand words about it, using all the precise verbs and adjectives and similes that come to mind. A kumquat is a citrus fruit, but there's something about it that's different from any other citrus fruit you've ever tried, and if you can't say what the difference is, you weren't concentrating hard enough. As for a persimmon, you can write a really interesting account if you get one that isn't ripe.

2. Make, knead, and bake a loaf of bread from scratch, using only flour, salt, water, and yeast. Find an old recipe and follow it. Concentrate on every step and sensation of it, and consider this most remarkable fact: The yeast is alive, like you, and is helping you make the bread. Try to imagine the first man (or woman) who ever baked a loaf, and saw dough rise, and smelled it. Imagine what thoughts went through the head of that original baker. There's a whole story of life in that, and when that happened, it was "now." It will also be now when you do it. After your bread is done, write everything you can express in words about the making of bread. Remember that in the old days, through the ages, people made bread; they didn't buy it at the supermarket. Your writing exercise about the loaf might end up someday in the appropriate place in a novel. In fact, anything you experience through your senses and write down might turn up in a novel. As I've been saying, life is research.

3. Describe everything about the experience of getting a mosquito bite. (If you've never had one, where have you been?)

4. Shut your eyes, sit or lie down in silence, and let your mind take you back to your very earliest conscious memory. Stay there with that memory and let it all rebuild: the pleasure, the scent, the noise, the heat, the cold, the pain if it was a painful moment—all the sensations of it. Most of it is still stored in your brain, even if you've never consciously recalled it. Then, when it's complete, start writing it, as if you were starting a book about your life, beginning at that moment, which was probably when you first became aware of your consciousness. The first memory account of a surprising proportion of my students was of being whipped or beaten by a parent.

    Some wrote that the first thing they remember was a Muppet or a Mouseketeer. That startled me. Having been a child long before television, I expected everyone's first conscious memory would have been of something real, not of a TV image.

5. The best, maybe hardest, sensuous writing exercise is this: Go to the thing you can't stand to think about—the most shameful, most painful, most horrifying, most embarrassing incident you've ever tried to forget—and start writing it. Face it and purge yourself of it on paper. You might lie at first; you might have to cry. Depending on how sheltered a life you have lived, it might just make you squirm or laugh at yourself. On the other hand, you might have been abused or assaulted sexually, or you might have committed something you consider a sin, or experienced some shameful moment of cowardice. Face it and go straight into it and describe it through the senses. You can probably write something through the senses that you couldn't stand to do as an emotional purge or a confession. But when you've written it through the senses, you've conquered your fear of looking straight at it.

I know a Vietnam veteran whose whole emotional life was warped and frozen around a ghastly moment, years and years ago, when his buddy was trapped in a burning armored vehicle and was begging to be shot and put out of his agony. The veteran was haunted by that moment for years and actually refused to remember whether he had shot him or not. He was going crazy with it. He couldn't shake hands, because his right hand had been his pistol hand. He was worthless. Finally he forced himself to write of the moment as a sense-assaulting combat narrative. I won't say what he wrote. But the writing of it changed his life. He now spends his life counseling traumatized veterans and has written books on how to bring them past their own torments. Facing that awful moment and writing it down restored a ruined life for the author himself.

The climax of a novel often is a moment that seems impossible to endure. If you can force yourself to exhume and record some personal horror you wanted to leave buried, then you will have trained yourself to write powerfully about anything the protagonist of your novel has to do.

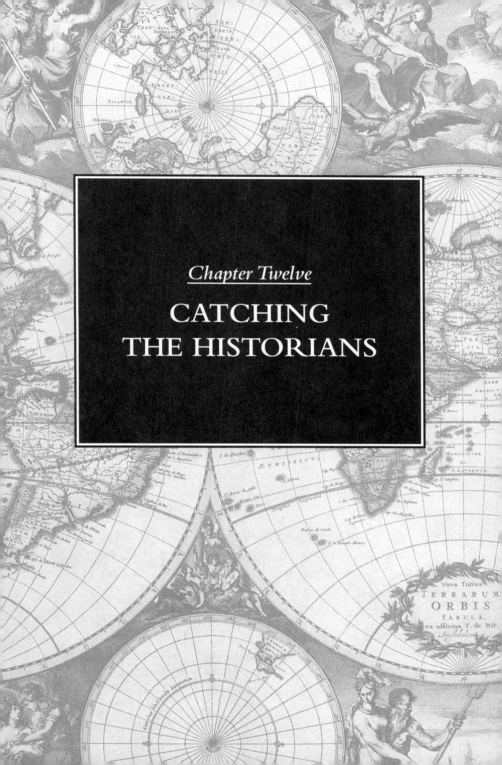

Chapter Twelve

CATCHING
THE HISTORIANS

ashington Irving once said, "History fades into fable."

The line between historical fact and fiction isn't always distinct. Here's a thought-provoking statement on that matter by the late Howard Zinn:

> Historical fiction and nonfiction are both abstractions from a complex world of infinite fact. Both can tell the truth; both can lie. The "lies" (that is, distortions, omissions, exaggerations) in historical fiction may have two advantages over the "lies" (that is, omissions, exaggerations, distortions) in nonfiction. First, that they are at least entertaining. Second, that they do not make the same claim of being truthful.
>
> The fact that historical fiction is more entertaining can also make it more dangerous, because it is more seductive, enveloping the lie in a sweeter package than nonfiction. Bad historical fiction may wrap a false idea (that blacks are inferior, that war is good) in an attractive story and thus make it more dangerous.

Historians believe that a major part of their responsibility is to keep history from fading into fable—that is, to keep a distinct line between truth and untruth—by constantly verifying and re-stating facts and dispelling the mist of myth and fable. We historical novelists, if we're good ones, honor them for that sense of responsibility, and we should strive to do the same thing, even while we're storytelling.

But another thing old Washington Irving said was, "I am always at a loss to know how much to believe of my own stories." A historian, if he spoke candidly, should admit the same doubt. However capable and conscientious he may be, he is a storyteller, just like you and me and Washington Irving.

In chapter 3, I introduced historian Stephen Ambrose, who inadvertently provoked me to write this book. When Stephen started working on a story about someone, whether it was an individual historical man or a military unit, he grew to be one in heart with his subject and became a passionate advocate. He had to struggle to remain objective about those whom he was learning to admire.

We're all subject to that weakness, of course. It's like falling in love.

Stephen's main realm of history was World War II, and a notable piece of that history was his work titled *Band of Brothers*. It was the history of one heroic company of the 101st Airborne and the men who served in it, becoming bonded into that sacred brotherhood of men who face death together over and over.

Band of Brothers was, deservedly, a rousing, inspiring success as a war history book, and eventually was adapted into a powerful and moving miniseries. Few critics had anything bad to say about the work itself, but some historian (I can't remember who) griped that the story made it seem that the band of brothers, that one unit, had won World War II all by themselves—that the millions of fighting men of other units and countries, including the more than seven million dead and wounded of the Soviet Union, hadn't had much to do with it.

In fairness to Stephen Ambrose, he wasn't writing about all the Allies; he was writing about that particular brave unit. But he did tend to get carried away.

In the realm of the American West, I found myself particularly bothered by the almost too idealized role of Captain Meriwether Lewis as portrayed in *Undaunted Courage*.

I, too, had studied and written about Lewis for many years. I knew that he was brilliant, brave, and visionary. But in at least one instance, I felt that Stephen had stretched reality a bit to make Lewis "politically correct" for modern readers, for example, when he declared that Captain Lewis had enabled a woman to vote for the very first time in American history. The woman was the Shoshone interpreter, Sacagawea.

Stephen Ambrose loved to believe that Lewis had done that commendable and significant deed, and here are the circumstances he
cited: Having reached the Pacific coast after an arduous 4,000-mile
trek, Lewis and Clark had to decide where their company would
bivouac for the winter. Though the officers had already decided on
a wooded site south of the Columbia River, sheltered from the direct force of the ocean but near enough that they would be aware if
trading ships came in, they decided to let their soldiers express their
opinions about what would be the best place to pass the winter.

This being a military unit, the officers didn't have to poll the
troops. But they had tried it once before, in discussing a route into
the Rocky Mountains, and it had seemed to be good for morale
when the men could express their opinions.

On the stormy coast in what's now the state of Washington,
Captain Lewis let the men state their reasons why they would pre-
fer one place or another, taking into consideration such factors as
climate, availability of fresh water and game, nearness to the sea-
shore or to particular Indian villages. Captain Clark made a written tally of their choices and their reasons. Not just the soldiers, but
the civilian hunter Drouillard, and even Clark's slave York, told of
their preferences. The interpreter Charbonneau, Sacagawea's husband, was listed, apparently having been asked, but stated no opinion. Sacagawea's name wasn't even in the tally.

Clark added them up. Almost unanimously, they were in agree-
ment with the captain's choice.

Left out of the poll, the young mother Sacagawea, who was their
main forager of vegetable provisions, spoke up to say she hoped they
would stay where she could harvest edible wapato roots.

Stephen Ambrose closed that section of his narrative with this
inspiring declaration: "It was the first time in American history that
a black slave had voted, the first time a woman had voted."

The historian was so proud to declare that his hero had made that vote possible! And soon, Lewis and Clark aficionados were echoing his statement with teary eyes and choked-up voices in their conversations and speeches everywhere along the bicentennial trail. It was really a "feel good" moment, a sweet touch of democracy in the American epic. It was as if Lewis were abolitionist, suffragist, and civil rights activist all at once, instead of the male white supremacist he actually was.

To me, this didn't make sense. Like the boy picking through puppy litters in Sharyn McCrumb's story, it didn't add up. I knew that Meriwether Lewis had a low regard for, and distrust of, Indians. He had written in his journal just that summer that Sacagawea probably had no thoughts or concerns of any consequence whatsoever.

It seemed to be up to me, a mere novelist, to be the spoilsport. So here was my reasoning, in four-part harmony:

1. No actual voting was done. The decision had already been made. The group of men had commented on the situation, nothing more. The word *vote* was nowhere mentioned in the journals.

2. It was commendable that the slave York had been allowed to speak on the matter. But out there, far from slave-holding Virginia society, he was temporarily almost as much an autonomous human being as any private soldier was. Like theirs, his opinion was not a real vote.

3. Sacagawea's opinion hadn't even been sought. The tally didn't list her name. She just spoke up saying she wanted to be where the vegetables grew. Hers was even more a non-vote than all the other non-votes, so it was really stretching to say she was the first woman in American history to vote.

4. Indian women in America had been voting for thousands of years, their votes equal to men's in tribal councils. In some tribes, women could even veto war plans or remove the chief if he wasn't doing a satisfactory job. It was *white* women who couldn't vote.

That was my argument, but it wasn't well taken. I had rained on the parade. Thereafter, if I was in a lecture audience when Dr. Ambrose described that long-ago forum at the mouth of the great Columbia River, he would stare straight at me while telling it the way he liked to. And in a later book, the commemorative edition printed by National Geographic upon release of its IMAX film of the expedition, he went even further to specify that it was the first time in American history that an *Indian* woman ever voted.

Sometimes a novelist's intuition, or imagination, seems to serve as well as research.

It seemed like another manifestation of this old problem: As far as white people are concerned, no history happened until they arrived and got involved in it.

You'd expect the *novelist* to be the one to embellish that scene into a stroke for women's suffrage, and the historian to refute such fancy with practical facts, instead of vice versa. And yet, I did understand Stephen's feelings perfectly. Years before, I had polished George Rogers Clark to a shine in the same way.

It's a small triumph for a historical novelist to trump the bona fide historians on some point of fact, but we do it now and then. (The historians don't have to admit it, so everybody's happy.)

In chapter 4, I first mentioned novelist Sharyn McCrumb and her rule of thumb that if the story doesn't make sense, keep looking. I asked Sharyn, "Do you think you've ever come closer to the essential truth than historians who've written of the same events and subjects?"

Her answer: "Essential truths, hell! At times, I got the facts right and they didn't!"

One case: In 1833 a mountain girl named Frankie Silver was hanged for murder in North Carolina. Two historians who wrote about the case interviewed some local residents in the 1990s and were told that Frankie Silver was hanged from a formal wooden trap-door style gallows. They said their grandparents remembered the hanging. Sharyn explains:

> Elderly people in 1990 claim their grandparents remembered an 1833 hanging? I don't think so. A trapdoor gallows in a small mountain town in 1833? I don't think so. So I did some general research, using three other legendary nineteenth-century hangings for comparison.

Those were Nat Turner, leader of a slave rebellion, Tom Dula ("Tom Dooley" of the ballad), and John Brown, the abolitionist.

In Frankie Silver's case, a pardon was expected, so the sheriff wasn't even sure he'd be hanging her, until the day of the execution. Would he build a fancy, costly gallows just in case?

The Virginia authorities knew they would be hanging Nat Turner, and had weeks to build a gallows, but instead they just strung him up from a high tree limb, using a ladder to get him up there.

In Tom Dula's case likewise; the execution was a foregone conclusion, and there were weeks to prepare for it, but Dula was simply made to stand in the back of a cart with the noose around his neck while the cart was driven out from under him. Still no trapdoor, even though this was thirty-four years after Frankie Silver's hanging and the technology could have been much advanced. That also took place in North Carolina. "I found it hard to

---

LOOKING UP THE NOSTRILS OF HISTORIANS

In the early 1960s, Dr. Vardis Fisher wrote a book titled, *Suicide or Murder? The Strange Death of Governor Meriwether Lewis.* It's an old argument that's still going on. As I write this, historians are gathering to continue the debate near the Tennessee location where Lewis died his violent death two hundred years ago. There are at least two new books out on the subject this year; I know both authors.

The debate in itself supports my repeated assertion in this book: that history isn't confined to the past, and that it's always in revision. Vardis Fisher's book didn't presume to answer its title question, but it did examine skeptically much of the "prevailing wisdom" on which the suicide theory was based. Fisher was so roundly attacked by Lewis and Clark scholars for even raising such doubts that another historian, John Guice, later testified: "I'm convinced that Vardis Fisher ... researched with incredible intensity and integrity, and I'm ashamed that some of my fellow scholars maligned him so. ... I suspect that one reason they did was that, though he was a Ph.D. in History, he did spend most of his career writing novels, and because he had written novels some of the historians have tried to look down their noses at his work."

If you become a historical novelist, expect to look up nostrils now and then. But the more conscientious your work, the less you'll have to do that.

---

believe," Sharyn says, "that a sheriff in a neighboring county, thirty-four years earlier, would have used a trapdoor gallows."

It's well known that John Brown was hanged from a state-of-the-art trapdoor gallows in 1859—not by a poor county sheriff, but by the Federal Government, with the Army Corps of Engineers building the gallows. "The only pre-1870s executions I could find using the trap-door gallows were those carried out by the government or the military," Sharyn says. "Small town county sheriffs, who might perform one execution a year, lacked the resources and the expertise to use such elaborate means. So, in my novel, I said Frankie Silver was hanged off the back of a cart, and I still say that the nonfiction historians who said otherwise were wrong."

Another astute fact-tracking historical novelist who finds things the historians have missed, or gotten wrong, is Lucia St. Clair Robson. She tells me:

> There are times when a generalist, like a novelist, uncovers more information than a specialist, precisely because he or she casts a wider net.
>
> I've often found information that historians have missed. For example, a Pulitzer Prize–winning biography of Andrew Jackson mentioned that Will Rogers was related to the Cherokee woman Tiana Rogers. Other researchers picked up on that "fact" and mentioned it in their nonfiction texts.

But Lucia had a doubt and tracked down the answer in the library at the University of Arkansas: Two men named John Rogers, one known as Nolichucky Jack and the other as Hell-Fire Jack, lived among the Cherokees at the same time, and the award-winning biographer had mixed them up. "Understandable," she says, "since the Cherokee were only a sidebar to his research."

....

[E]ven the most objective historian has an axe to grind. It's part of his motivation. He may try to be totally unbiased, but a certain degree of bias gives him the impetus to start in one direction.

....

Sometimes a novelist's intuition, or imagination, seems to serve as well as research. Lucia tells me:

> I received a call from a Cherokee descendant of Hell-Fire Jack Rogers. She said the family wanted to know where I had gotten the stories in *Walk in My Soul*, the novel I had written about them.

> I said I had either read them or made them up. She said, 'No, you
> couldn't have. Those are stories only the family knows.'

That story of Lucia's struck a chord with me. When I was writing
my historical novel *Sign-Talker*, I included a Nez Perce tribal chief
whose name intrigued me, and I wondered how he had gotten that
name. It was Cutnose.

The name *Nez Perce* is French, meaning "pierced nose," which
might have explained it, except that the tribe's name for itself wasn't
Nez Perce, it was Nimipu. Presuming I'd never have a way of knowing for certain, nor that anyone could prove I was wrong, I imagined
an intertribal fight in which a wound would have earned him that
name, and I imagined it in detail. It was a fight that well might have
happened, according to the tribal histories of those conflicts.

Soon after I'd written that scene, the Lewis and Clark bicentennial activities put me in touch with a Nez Perce tribal historian who, I discovered, was a direct descendant of Cutnose. I asked
him whether he knew how the chief had come by that name. He
did know, and as he described the fight, my scalp began to prickle: Every detail of the story was just as I had imagined it—weapon,
setting, everything. Somehow, in my mind's eye, I had seen something that really did happen, more than two hundred years ago.
I'm not making this up.

Well, then, maybe Stephen Ambrose had a vision into the past
that same way and heard Captain Lewis say, "Hey! It's not right
that women and slaves can't vote! Let's fix that, Captain Clark!
Prepare the ballots!"

But I don't think so.

AN AXE TO GRIND

Even the most objective historian starts a project with some degree of subjectivity: He selects the topic, and he has a notion of the

case he will make. If he didn't have a point he wanted to make, he wouldn't start a project—unless he was assigned, say, to write a history project on a particular time and place, as a historian for hire, with strict parameters set by the official curriculum.

In other words, even the most objective historian has an axe to grind. It's part of his motivation. He may try to be totally unbiased, but a certain degree of bias gives him the impetus to start in one direction.

Sometimes a historian has a nagging discontent about what he feels is the wrong official slant, and decides to add to or modify the perspectives, in order to help the reading public understand something better. This is not always good, but sometimes it is an excellent thing to do, perhaps long overdue. The finest example I know of is Howard Zinn's classic, *A People's History of the United States,* which I've mentioned. To my mind, it is the most important American history book written in the last century.

Howard, who had researched and taught history, had gotten involved in civil rights and antiwar movements, coming to these conclusions about "official" American history:

> Behind every fact presented to the world ... is a judgment. The judgment that has been made is that this fact is important, and that other facts, omitted, are not important.
>
> There were themes of profound importance to me which I found were missing in the orthodox histories that dominated American culture. The consequence of those omissions has been not simply to give a distorted view of the past but, more important, to mislead us all about the present.

And so he wrote a history book about many of the things that had been omitted because they were so unpleasant to remember: genocide of the American Indians, indentured servitude, slavery, exploitation of labor, military aggression, imperialism, class warfare, religious prejudice, nativism, corporatism, and the relentless undercurrent of corruption.

I could not write this book of mine without speaking of the importance of Howard's work credo, because I have come to believe that this kind of "alternative" realm of history is one place where historical novelists can do very much good, dispelling what has become the official myth. I, myself, came to this view by outgrowing the Teddy Roosevelt mindset.

Much of my fan mail comes from readers who exclaim that they never knew the "other side of that story." They write to me and say, "Finally, that makes sense!" Or, "Really, General Harrison was more asshole than hero, wasn't he?"

And one of the best lessons I ever taught by writing a novel, I guess, is acknowledged by readers who say such things as, "It's obvious to me for the first time that Lewis and Clark couldn't have succeeded in their glorious expedition without the generosity, cooperation, and guidance of the Indians they met all along the way. What an eye-opener!"

When *A People's History* was first published in 1980, it was a revelation to most people who thought they knew America's story. Not surprisingly, it upset many. "Some reviewers," Howard told me, "characterized my history as 'un-American,' because they believed I was overemphasizing the flaws in U.S. policy and actions. The veracity of my historical writing has often been challenged— mostly by people hostile to my point of view .... Disputes over fundamental points of view will remain unresolved."

When he started writing his book, he had judged that those disturbing topics were too important to remain absent from American history. Howard was a patriot all his life—a life he often put on the line—and he believed that loving one's country requires a full knowledge of the country as it really has been, and is, warts and all.

The reason why those ugly aspects of history have to be known is that they helped make this country what it is; we are constantly recycling the mistakes of our past, and we are what we are because of what our forebears did. Many of the conflicts we have in the world today are hard for us to understand, because our national past has been prettified and ennobled in our education. The rest of the world has studied us, the good and the bad. This country is admired for its greatness, but is also envied for it, and hated for its smugness—a smugness we wouldn't have if we knew ourselves better.

One of the chapters in his *People's History* concerned the U.S.-Mexican War of 1846–48. He believed it was an unprovoked, imperialist war of aggression, with consequences lasting into the present, and that by glossing over it in our history books, we fail to understand the roots of our present border problems. He believed also that if Americans knew how that war was started, we would resist letting our leaders start invasions like that of Iraq in 2003. When he learned that I was writing a novel about the U.S.-Mexican War, he encouraged me. "Good historical fiction lends a special passionate intensity to truths which you may find in historical nonfiction in a more bland, and therefore less powerful, form," he said. "Telling it through fascinating characters and a story you get involved in gives it more power."

When a historian of Howard Zinn's stature and intellect says that our historical fiction can serve a good purpose, we can feel that perhaps we do have some validity. I asked him if he had ever considered writing in the genre.

"Yes, in fact," he replied. "I once wrote a historical novel based on the Ludlow Massacre in Colorado in 1914. I decided then that I don't have the gifts of a good novelist, and I abandoned it after it was rejected by a number of publishers. Eventually, I decided they were right to reject it."

He was successful in another genre, however: plays. Two of them, one, *Emma,* about Emma Goldman, the other *Marx in Soho,* have been staged far and often. But even those plays are history lessons that are hard to find anywhere else.

Remember, when we're considering how we'll tell history, working conscientiously, we will get our facts as correct as we can. That's a paramount responsibility we have to those who might learn any history from us.

But we will have an axe to grind, a reason to tell the story, and we'll choose according to who we are and what we've done. Howard Zinn refers to himself as a "partisan," and avers that his partisanship was shaped by his working-class, soldiering life, as well as his studies.

I was one in a long line of dutiful soldiers, but under my mother's Quaker-based influence, a career in journalism, and immersion in Mark Twain's amused skepticism, I developed a B.S. filter and a desire to seek what truthful stories might run unseen under the official narratives. So now I am an American storyteller leaning toward peacemakers and underdogs, and more Indian than cowboy. Teddy Roosevelt would have been disappointed in me. That's fine with me.

You might take an entirely different route. Who you are will determine what axe you'll choose to grind. That's as it should be. The more you live, the better you'll write.

That can play hell with your objectivity. But may the facts keep you honest.

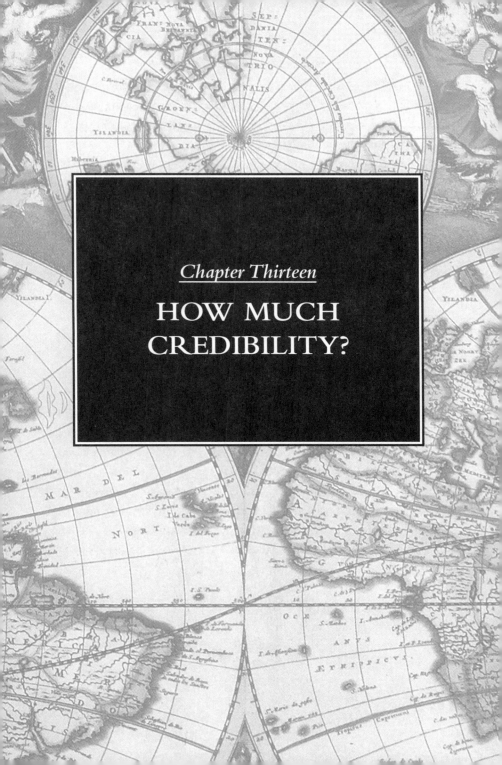

Chapter Thirteen

HOW MUCH CREDIBILITY?

he hardest question for a historical novelist to answer, on those rare occasions when a reader is bold enough to ask it, is this one: "In your novels, where does the history stop and the fiction begin?"

A hard question to answer, but I'm always glad to hear it asked, because it means that someone cares about historical truth. The answer is, basically, this: The history doesn't stop. It's there from the first page to the last, and it's as accurate as my research can make it. The fiction begins where my research can't find or verify any more facts.

But even where the research has run out, I remain in pursuit of the truth. Remember that word verisimilitude? With whatever intelligence, imagination, and instinct I have, I write for verisimilitude. If it seems true, it might be. If it doesn't seem true, it probably isn't.

Savvy readers of historical fiction know that the dialogue in a historical novel almost certainly was made up. They know that there weren't recording devices in those days. And even if there's historical documentation that an encounter or a discussion did occur, there's seldom a verbatim record of what was said. Depositions were hardly ever taken, even though varieties of stenography, or shorthand, have been in use since the days of Caesar, and an alphabet-based technique was invented in Queen Elizabeth's lifetime. Few actual conversations were taken down verbatim. So you don't see dialogue in nonfiction history. But novels *need* dialogue.

Although we historical novelists weren't there to hear what historical figures did say to each other, our research can show us what they'd have discussed. Their letters and journals tell us what they had on their minds, what they thought about events and issues. One of the problems that President Jefferson had to deal with, as

American President Obama did in 2009, was African pirates who were attacking and seizing American ships. So, if there's a scene in a novel in which our hero is on an American sailing ship in the Mediterranean Sea in 1804, it's very likely that he and the ship's captain would talk about the topic of piracy, and they might well talk of Jefferson's anti-piracy policy. That would be especially likely if our hero happened to be young Lieutenant Presley O'Bannon of the Marines. That dashing youth, a Virginian and a decent fiddle player, eventually led a few Marines on a swift, successful shore mission against the pirate base at Tripoli. It's the origin of "the shores of Tripoli" in "The Marine Corps Hymn," in case you've not deduced it yet.

The point here is that, knowing O'Bannon, knowing why the American ship is over there, knowing Jefferson's intent and the ship captain's orders—all of which we know from our research to be factual—it's very, very likely that the two officers had a conversation about what they would be doing about pirate attacks, and the author of this historical novel could create a tense, detailed dialogue between the two officers about how to take the fight to the pirates. There is your verisimilitude. It wouldn't make sense if they *didn't* have such a conversation.

On the other hand, if young O'Bannon in the novel got caught up in a love affair with a lovely belly dancer while he was over there, that likely would be fiction (although who knows about those Marines!), and the author would certainly be free to make up their conversations, which probably would not be about Jefferson's foreign policy.

Even in that case, though, a good historical novelist would do some research to find out about belly dancers of that time, including some notion of what one of them might want to murmur about during pillow talk with the lieutenant. Even love scenes need some dialogue, beyond "Oooh! Oh! Aaaahhh!" and "Was it good for you, too?"

The history doesn't stop. It's there from the first page to the last, and it's as accurate as my research can make it. The fiction begins where my research can't find or verify any more facts.

A historian writing about Lieutenant O'Bannon in those circumstances could pause in his account and say, "There is no documented evidence of a rumor among his troops that the Marine officer had romantic liaisons with a noted Libyan dancer." Or he could put that in a footnote. But the historical novelist can't fudge like that, and must choose whether to give the lieutenant his dalliance, or never bring it up. Most novel-readers probably would expect to see a love story, and they might wonder where the history left off and the fiction began, but wouldn't really care.

In the course of a novel, I have to imagine and create meetings, social events, dining occasions, strolls, idylls, arguments, tasks, and many other incidents in the lives of my characters—incidents of which there is no historical record, not even a note in any diary or memoir. I take the liberty of writing such scenes, because they were common in the lives of those people in those times, and they serve as settings for the advancement of the story, or to show important sites, to demonstrate character traits, to show how things were done in those days, to involve my reader in those lives, in a natural way, without altering or interfering with any of the recorded history.

Whether some particular incident ever happened, no one knows, but I know such incidents did happen in the lives of my characters. Without such scenes and the conversations that took place there and then, my narrative would proceed through a vacuum. A good portion of the scenes in any historical novel are fictional—that is, created by the author's imagination—but so likely to have happened that they aren't necessarily untrue.

In brief, that answers the question, where does history end and fiction begin.

TOO MUCH CREDIBILITY?

After working through much of my writing career trying to maintain a high degree of credibility, I have lately been brought up short and made uneasy by an instance or two of what might be deemed "too much credibility." I mentioned before the reader who Googled my fictional character Dr. Case from the novel *Warrior Woman*, presuming he had been a real person. That was a minor incident, which did no harm.

In another instance, "too much credibility" had a consequence I regret, and it's not my pleasure to write of it here, but I shall, because there's a lesson in it.

In fleshing out the protagonist of my novel *Sign-Talker*, George Drouillard, the Shawnee mixed-breed hunter and interpreter for Lewis and Clark, I gave him something many Native Americans have: a secret name by which individuals characterize their true selves, in addition to the known names they answer to. Since no one, including myself, could ever know what his private name was, I was free to make one up, an appropriate one, such as he well might have chosen for himself, and no historical nitpicker could ever prove that he hadn't thought of himself by that name.

Genealogical and other research had filled me in on everything that was known of his life before the explorers hired him, and all that was documentable "true history." The name I imagined he would secretly call himself was where the fiction entered the picture, and I came by it through what I call "informed intuition," like this:

Born too late to have been involved in his people's resistance to the white men's invasion of their territory, he believed that he would never have a chance to earn a warrior's eagle feather for bravery in battle. In that regard, he chose a name that dealt with that relative lack of self-esteem. With due respect for his departed spirit, I took the liberty of having him think of himself as Nah S'gawateah Kindiwa, meaning "Without Eagle Feathers."

I took some risk in devising that name. Much of the Shawnee language has been lost, and good translations are hard to come by. The few living Shawnees still fluent in their old tongue might dispute it, but so far I haven't heard from them.

Modern Shawnee Indians generally took to that book, by what I've heard, as Drouillard really was a credit to his people. One Shawnee band in Oklahoma seized the opportunity to mint and nationally advertise a George Drouillard memorial coin during the years of the Lewis and Clark Bicentennial, a coin bearing his image which they lifted from the artwork on the dust-jacket of my novel. On the obverse of the coin were more figures taken from the dust-jacket. Those Shawnees didn't bother to ask permission to use the artwork, and some of my white acquaintances thought that I or my publisher should raise a fuss about that. Shouldn't we share the profit they'd make using our images on their coins?

Most white folks think that way. In fact, if it had been white men who minted that coin, I might have made a fuss over it. But I was happy to see the Shawnees get a rare opportunity to make a few bucks, and their coin didn't detract any from my publisher's profitability, or mine. In their advertisement for their coin they used historical facts from my book, none fictional. No harm done.

Besides that, I had taken Shawnee persons, Drouillard, Tecumseh, and Nonhelema, without asking any Shawnee permission, and made novels about their lives, which have earned money to put food on my table for a long time. And some of that money has also put food on Shawnee tables. Indians have always fed me, and I'll always feed them.

If you become a historical novelist, be as accurate as you can be, but don't declare to the world that you can't be doubted.

This is their country, anyway. The rest of us have just been visiting here, and not very grateful guests, at that. The Shawnee band is welcome to borrow my images of their person.

Getting back to Nah S'gawateah Kindiwa and too much credibility: An Indian friend of mine in Ohio, respected as an amateur historian and a genealogist of Indian families, wrote in a reference tract about Drouillard's fictional private name that meant "Without Eagle Feathers," and he spelled it out and presented it as fact. That startled me.

As soon as I had a chance to speak to him, I told him that Drouillard's secret name was a fictional invention, for my novel, and that he should retract it from his work. I could see the surprise and disappointment in his face. "But we suppose everything you write to be true," he said.

I realized then that he meant not just Shawnees, but many of my non-Indian readers. Who knows how many of them just mix the facts and the fiction together in their minds? Since book reviewers and even historians often testify as to the historical accuracy of my novels, there might well be readers out there who accept even the fictional details of my novels as truths. The printed designation—"A Novel"—on the cover doesn't necessarily make them immune to believing it all.

That would be no big problem if confined to people's perceptions and inner thoughts. But when they relay fictions as facts into print, either on paper or on the Internet, they inadvertently spread what may be misinformation because of something I invented. Then it might turn up on a school paper written by a student who gets his data off the Web.

That's why I called this problem "too much credibility."

AND WAY TOO MUCH CREDIBILITY

I've long been aware of the hazard of "too much credibility," having learned of it through the tragic case of a famous historical novelist of recent decades. It's embarrassing to admit it, but I myself was misled by his credibility, and it was a long time before I knew it.

I won't speak of him by name out of respect for the deceased. But I will tell his story, because it is a powerful cautionary tale that could keep aspiring historical novelists from making historical mistakes.

That novelist was a prodigious researcher and a prolific writer. He wrote of great events and conflicts on the American frontier east of the Mississippi, novels of vast scope, interweaving the careers of famous frontiersmen, Indians, generals, and politicians. His books were very successful, because they showed the big pictures of frontier warfare and settlement. They taught much history in exciting, awe-inspiring, and often violent narratives that one could read over and over. He wrote about men and events that had been almost forgotten, and for some decades did it so well that he had a virtual monopoly on the genre for those periods and regions. I was one of his many readers, and I learned many facts from them.

I was learning in those days to be a historical novelist. Some of the frontiersmen and the Indians I was writing about had appeared in his sagas, and he had already made them come alive for me. I trusted his stories and was inspired by him to be as thorough and reliable a researcher as he was.

He seemed to be a marvelous combination of novelist and historian. Unlike mere novels, his epics contained indexes and bibliographies, as well as copious end notes in which he discussed his sources. And he stated in the beginning that although his books were novels, everything in them was true and could be verified in his research references.

But an odd thing began happening: As I researched my own Indian war stories, often running into the same archives and sources he had used, I sometimes found that I wasn't drawing the same inferences as he had. Now and then, some document he had cited as proof of something actually didn't seem to prove it at all, and might even contradict it. I knew, of course, that inferences are often influenced by one's own expectations and personal biases.

Then I found that certain cited references within this or that archive weren't really there. Now and then I would meet some local historian who would try to tell me that the great author had made something up, or had twisted a reference to make his story more dramatic, or to cover up some discrepancy elsewhere. Such things a historical novelist understandably might do, but not if he has declared that everything in his book is historically factual.

I didn't want to hear what those nitpickers were saying, of course, but I was beginning to discover little things that gnawed at my faith in his credibility.

One of my favorite minor scenes in one of his novels related an amusing incident in which an Indian leader expressed contempt for a white trader by backing up to him and farting loudly

BUT, IF IT SELLS ...

"God! All that research!" you might exclaim about now, and ask, "What's wrong with writing sexy, flamboyant, fantastic historical fiction right out of my imagination, if that's what some readers want, and that's where the money is?" (In other words, the kind of factless fiction Steve Ambrose alluded to.)

That's a valid question, I have to admit, even though it runs counter to my message in this book.

It's true, many readers aren't looking for authenticity and realism, they're looking for romantic adventure, for swordfighters in tight pants, for pneumatic bosoms flushed with passion, for palace intrigues, for poison drops in wine goblets. To such readers, the past is a place to escape to, from a humdrum present.

A good blurb from a respected historian isn't what they look for on a book's cover; they look for cleavage, moistened lips, bejeweled daggers. I'm glad to see people buy and read even that kind of historical novels. They're reading. They're at least thinking about earlier times. They're keeping their imaginations alive.

If you want to write that kind of historical fiction, you probably will. It might be fun and even profitable, and I congratulate any writer who has fun and gets paid. Much of the world's historic lore is myth, anyway.

Meanwhile, we who research hard and write conscientiously and authentically, we will hope that now and then one of your readers, initiated into some historical era or subject by your work, will begin wondering what it was really like back then, will begin yearning for verisimilitude, for the real significance of some bygone event. I've heard from many readers who say they came to me that way.

There are even real historians whose readers' curiosity was first piqued by something they saw in a bodice-ripper.

in his face. It was in character for that particular Indian, and was a vivid, bawdy scene. It seemed like something a novelist would invent, but a real historian wouldn't write. The incident served in the novel to ridicule a foolish American trader named Jethro Fischer, a Kentuckian, at a time when the Indian hated and distrusted American whites. Thus the scene had verisimilitude, making sense as well as scents.

But when I found the primary source of the scene, a page handwritten by the trader himself, lo and behold, the trader wasn't named Jethro at all, he was Frederick Fisher, and he wasn't Kentuckian but British. The novelist had changed him, for effect. In ensuing years, I found so many little twists and embellishments, I lost any desire I'd ever had to meet the great novelist, because he would know from my versions of those stories that I was onto him, and that would be embarrassing.

Sometimes I would try to verify his version of some story and find that the verifiers themselves had accepted his version as fact. I asked several "authorities," both white and Indian, about one major circumstance in one of his novels, because it didn't seem to make sense under the circumstances, and it seemed romanticized. A source I trusted, one who had popped a couple of mythic bubbles for me already, assured me that this yarn was true. So did other sources, who cited other accounts that upheld the novelist's version. I went to those accounts, and they did agree, so I wrote my version, published in one of my novels, and it was largely in accord with his. Years later, I found an obscure scholarly refutation of that romanticized version, and realized that I had been taken in; I, too, had perpetuated a myth in my novel.

You see, the "other accounts" that upheld his version had been written by authors who had believed him because he averred that all he wrote was true. The novelist had started the false version—

perhaps choosing to believe it himself—and it kept recirculating. The novelist himself kept recirculating it, and when his yarn began to unravel under scholarly scrutiny, he defiantly held to it. It was a long time before he conceded that he himself had been fooled by some old inaccurate accounts that had seemed believable, and he had sustained that version for decades.

Many of his myths are still out there, believed by readers who haven't kept up with the disavowals. That old novelist and I share many fans because we covered the same historical period, and sometimes I'm the one who has to break the bad news to those readers. I try to do it without diminishing his whole reputation, and, if I can, I explain how he erred. That means I have to explain also now and then how I erred, in believing him and not verifying quite far enough.

I still respect that old novelist for all the good history he taught so vividly. I surely have some readers who would never have looked into my novels if he hadn't already hooked them on the subjects and the genre. When I finally met him, I didn't mention our difference. Neither did he. We just spoke as polite peers. I'm glad because he died a few weeks later.

I'm grateful to him for this lesson I obtained from his embarrassment, this "too much credibility" lesson I'm passing on to you: If you become a historical novelist, be as accurate as you can be, but don't declare to the world that you can't be doubted.

As a novelist, you won't be able to pause in the middle of your story and say, "There are different versions of this, the first being that ..." Say, for example, the scene is the moment in the morning of April 15, 1865, when Abraham Lincoln, his head on the blood-soaked pillow, is declared dead, and Secretary of War Edwin Stanton murmurs the dramatic, sad remark: "Now he belongs to the ages." Or he might say, "Now he belongs to the angels."

The men standing in the room weren't sure. A historian could explain that doubt, or make a footnote of it. But you the novelist can't do that. Whichever version you write is what your reader will hear him say.

If you're a really conscientious novelist, though, and are afraid that you have attained too much credibility to be doubted, there's still an escape hatch for you: After the end of your novel, you can follow up with an "Author's Note" section, and discuss any such equivocations, thereby answering that question, *Where does the history end and the fiction begin?*

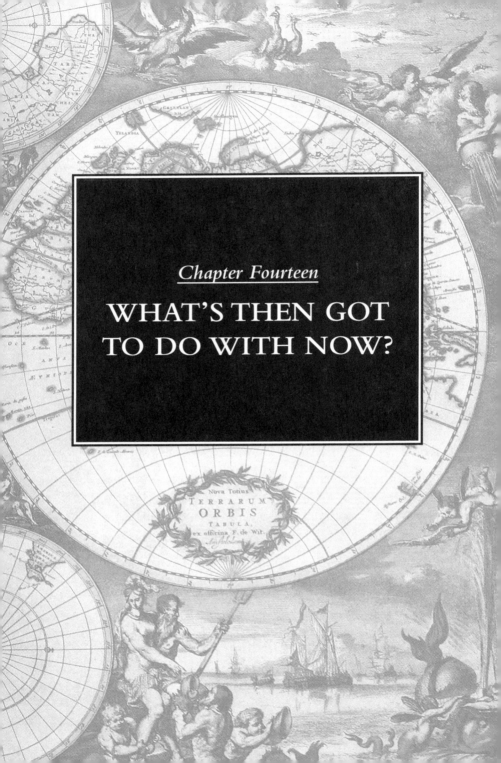

Chapter Fourteen

WHAT'S THEN GOT TO DO WITH NOW?

istorical fiction is, for many readers, an escape from the troubles and complexities of the present. But its readers don't necessarily want to escape from reality into fantasy. The past they hope to visit is not the mythical past of the Shire or Narnia, with flying dragons and orcs and Hobbits, but the past of this real world. It's the time they want to change, not the reality.

Readers like these are open to real historical truths, real civilizations, real significance. They might be drawn to James Clavell's *Shogun*, or Paul Scott's *The Raj Quartet*, or Cormac McCarthy's *Blood Meridian*, in which they will be immersed in stories about real times and places as they were. By reading stories of the real past, they will come to understand more about how the modern world became what it is. That's important for anyone to know, because, as I said, we are living with consequences.

MORTMAIN, THAT'S WHAT

Mortmain is an old French word that should be tattooed on the inside of any historical novelist's skull. This wonderful and terrible word means "dead hand." Its definition is: "The influence of the past regarded as controlling the present." (It is also used as a legal term with the same basic meaning.)

Everything a historical novelist writes is weighted with *mortmain*, because, as I keep emphasizing, consequences are forever being created. The hands that signed the Magna Carta, the Declaration of Independence, the Louisiana Purchase, the Emancipation Proclamation, and the United Nations Charter are all dead hands now, but we live in a world they shaped. Likewise, the hands that cut down old forests, and shot the bison herds and the last of the passenger pigeons, and released atomic bombs on Hiroshima and Nagasaki are dead now, as are the hands that piloted airliners to hit the World Trade Center towers in September, 2001. But we are all living with those consequences, too. The dead hand of history is always upon us. *Mortmain* would have been an appropriate title for this book. You, as a historical storyteller, might be the voice who can make this *mortmain* concept apparent to readers.

....

A historical novelist with an eye to the real importance of cause and effect might take any esoteric knowledge or forgotten deed and put it into a rousing story, giving modern readers an understanding of something that will affect us now, or soon in the future.

....

Clavell's *Shogun* examined a culture in old Japan, a system of military governorship and an elaborate code of honor unlike anything else in history. The novels examine that. The history of Japan is important to us for many reasons, from the old vicious enmity after Pearl Harbor, through our incendiary and atomic bombing of its cities, and General Douglas MacArthur's postwar administration that led to the financial and political alliance we have with that country now. Japan's history is a huge and significant part of America's history. It happened as it did because of the shogun influence, even though that system ended in the nineteenth century.

The Raj, meaning "reign," in India is likewise a historical point we need to understand, because India's history is interwoven with ours, through World War II and into the precarious present, in which that country is, like America, a nuclear power. We haven't heard the end of those consequences. And chances are, you might have noticed how often businesses outsource work to companies located in India. One part of the making of modern India is the astonishing fact that the Indian man who forced England to give In-

FEATHERS IN THE WIND

Believe it or not, in some societies, a murderer might be forgiven, but a gossip put to death.

In a Shawnee Indian story, one woman became so jealous of another that she started a false rumor about her. When she began to see the terrible effects of her gossip, she was sorry, and asked for her forgiveness.

"I will forgive you only if you can do this," that woman said. "Go now everywhere in the village and lay a feather outside each door.

"A year from now, go through the village again and gather up all the feathers. If you can bring back every single feather, I can forgive you for the lie you told about me."

The moral of that story is that gossip, like feathers in the wind, can never be fully called back.

Pocvano madeeweh—false gossip—is considered by some Shawnees a more serious crime than murder. Murder kills the body just once; gossip keeps killing the real person—the spirit—for as long as people remember. You would have to atone for murder, in some serious manner, but you probably wouldn't be executed. If your gossip killed someone's good name, it was likely a capital offense.

Such cultural values astonish and bewilder people who look in from other cultures, but yet seem strangely sensible enough to make one's scalp prickle. To write well about historical events anywhere in this vast, diverse world of peoples, you must research all the mores and traditions that make the cultures. Until you've done that, you aren't ready to write a story occurring in that place ... once upon a time.

dia its independence in the twentieth century organized a system of nonviolent social resistance that grew out of a nineteenth century American writer's essay, "Civil Disobedience." That writer, Henry David Thoreau, went to jail for his conscientious refusal to pay a tax that would help fund the U.S. invasion of Mexico, and his essay later influenced the passive resistance idea that Mahatma Gandhi put into nationwide action to throw off British rule of India. That is a wondrous testimony to the power of an idea to change the world.

As I said in the beginning of this book, all events run as tributaries into the River of History. As result, the now-dead writing hand of one solitary, quirky author in New England was eventually used by millions of desperately poor people in India to change the world. The same written idea also became the basic technique of Martin Luther King Jr. in the Civil Rights movement. And it goes on even now, as crowds protest against wars and socioeconomic injustices. Thoreau's hand is a *mortmain*, but it wrote words that still influence us now and will continue to do so.

A historical novelist with an eye to the real importance of cause and effect might take any esoteric knowledge or forgotten deed and put it into a rousing story, giving modern readers an understanding of something that will affect us now, or soon in the future. An example that came to mind not long ago was a statement by the president of Iran, who told an audience at Columbia University, "In Iran, we don't have homosexuals like in your country."

Oh, really? Iran used to be Persia. A novelist with the slightest exposure to Persian history, literature, Sufi poetry, and so on, might be challenged by that statement to write a juicy and intriguing novel based on the Persian traditions of bisexual love and the keeping of pretty boys, or about the romantic attachment of women and girls within the harem and without, within and between social classes, or about all the intricate codes of homoerotic behavior that were acceptable through the centuries in that land. It was only in the twentieth century that homophobia spread to that part of the world from the West. If President Ahmadinejad really believed what he said in that speech, the real facts of life in Iran must be hidden in a very well-sealed closet. If that great, rich old nation is hiding a nuclear weapons development project, as our political leaders keep warning us, it's not the only thing they're hiding. The president's smug remark almost dared someone to write a certain kind of historical novel.

Any place or any time you go to for your historical novel, you will be faced with your own ignorance of the past. You might know one fact that is intriguing enough to make you want to write your novel; that's what will compel you to start. But you have to be very humble about your knowledge and set out to overcome your ignorance. Before you're ready to tell that story well, you might have to study and learn the equivalent of an entire specialized college education on the society in which your story takes place, because all sorts of things were happening that you need to understand before you can even begin to tell a story in that milieu.

My wife, who is a natural scholar, has studied the Mayan culture of Central America, off and on, for a long time. Years ago, she toured some of the old city sites and temples, and these places took a strong hold on her fancy. Now, for the last few weeks, she has been nose-deep in concentrated reading about the Mayans. If she observed me doing the same, she would have reason to say, "So, your next novel is going to be about the Mayans?" It would be a good guess, too, as those are the first symptoms of the growth of a novel in me. Neither of us is planning to write a novel about the Mayans in the near future. But she and I are both reading about them, and it's not out of the question that one or both of us might write such a novel eventually. We might even co-author such a novel, if a theme or plot grows vivid enough to drive us in that direction.

I'm reading about Mayans in a particular context: the mysterious, sudden, and total collapse of their powerful and intricate civilization and the sociological and environmental causes of it. She's studying their mythology and prophecies, including their prophecies of doom. Obviously there's some overlap in those two mysteries. She and I are old enough that it's natural for us to be thinking about the end of things. Certain factors make civilizations fail, and historians recognize those factors when they show up in the present. Historical novelists should do likewise. A novel taking place in the last days of the Mayan kingdoms could be a colorful, powerful, and exotic story about war, religion, gold, and cannibalism. It could be full of portent and educate readers about a little-known age of the American past.

And in the telling, it could help readers recognize modern environmental and sociological parallels with the fates of old, failed civilizations. Such a novel would be enlightening and useful, not just an entertaining epic. It could maybe even be prophetic.

Or if you identify with macho white-guy adventure, try the Vikings. Those guys looked like something out of Xtreme Kombat, with mustaches almost as gigantic as their muscles, with bared teeth and wild eyes, horns on their helmets, leather vests studded with nails, a Hell's Angels attitude, and a thirst for beer. They swashbuckled out of Scandinavia in swift, seaworthy longboats (literally: their bucklers—shields—were hung on the vessels' gunwales where they were wet by the swash of the sea), and they terrorized the inhabitants in every Anglo-Saxon civilization. They took over islands as small as the Shetlands and as large as Greenland, carried off fainting damsels, and ripped their bodices. Their story has every kind of action, and all the "Saxon violence" you could crave.

But their reign of terror was brief in terms of human history, just a few short centuries, and therein, perhaps, lies the significant part of their saga; there's where it becomes meaningful in the mainstream of history. When and why did those rambunctious raiders settle down, marry up with their swooning captive women, devote themselves to herding cows, sheep, and pigs, and eventually abandon most of their conquered outposts? For the fact is, that's just what they did. Climatologists and archaeologists have collected evidence that the Vikings quit raiding when they ran out of convenient places to raid profitably, and then abandoned their settlements after deforesting and overgrazing the environs, or when the Eskimoan peoples got tired of having them around.

Any place or any time you go to for your historical novel, you will be faced with your own ignorance of the past. ... [Y]ou have to be very humble about your knowledge and set out to overcome your ignorance.

To those of us who like to consider history in the big picture, the Vikings' quiet demise is as interesting as their rowdy onslaught. This interest is because of the "scope" of a story I spoke of in chapter 5: its significance, its causes and effects, which both precede and follow the story's beginning and ending.

What's most important about Mayan and Viking history is that defunct civilizations can show us how our own might perish. Pride, conflict, profligacy, and environmental recklessness brought many old civilizations to ruin, and now our whole globe is infected with the same old syndrome. Historical novelists, if we're serious enough about it and concerned enough with the scope of our tales, can help illuminate the path into the future. That's because, though we're focusing toward the past, we're also looking forward.

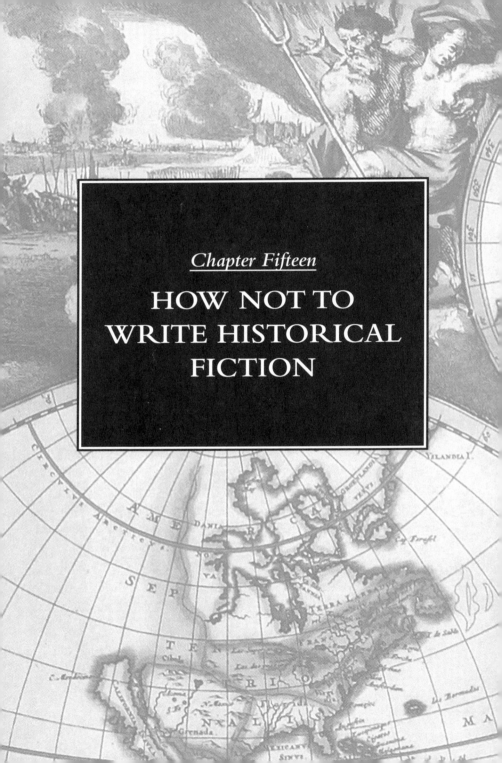

Chapter Fifteen

HOW NOT TO
WRITE HISTORICAL
FICTION

ooking up people's nostrils is a bad viewpoint. To avoid it, try not to give them cause to look *down* their noses at you: Don't write *bad* historical fiction.

That has been my urgent admonition throughout this book, you notice.

To amplify that message, I invited some esteemed historians to explain what they deem bad historical fiction, the kind they might look at down their noses.

"Bad historical fiction can be, first of all, just bad fictional writing," says Dayton Duncan, American historical author and screenwriter for some of the great Ken Burns history documentaries on public television. He continues:

> But even worse, it can distort the historical record (or even contradict it) in a misguided desire to make the past "more dramatic." I think too many historical novelists operate on the mistaken belief that history has to be gussied up—and they go out of the way in the service of supposedly making their story more dramatic.
>
> On the other hand, the best historical novels—and I've read quite a few of them—understand that history already has the raw material of drama, and concentrate instead on deepening our appreciation, even clarifying our understanding of it, without rearranging the basic facts ....
>
> The best nonfiction and fiction share many traits, the most obvious being compelling prose and a narrative that brings the reader along. Fiction takes the skeleton of historical fact and, without changing that structure, adds flesh, muscle, organs, and most of all, the breath of spirit.

He knows what he's talking about. Dayton Duncan's own approach to historical research and writing is one of body and soul. Whether writing or lecturing, he is a lump-in-the-throat, tear-in-the-eye storyteller—deeply moved by what real people have done and endured.

To reach that state of sensitivity, he researches the way I tell you to do: by undergoing the experience. Dayton has slept under a buffalo robe on subzero North Dakota nights, and retraced the footsteps of human heroes through vast, rugged landscapes.

"Historical fiction, when it's done well," he tells me, "is a wonderful addition to our understanding of the past. When it's done badly, I think it's trash and sometimes even dangerous to the purposes of telling history."

English historian John Sugden echoes Dayton Duncan's thoughts on the genre, explaining:

> Bad historical fiction, apart from the obvious conclusion that it simply may be bad fiction in itself, fails to evoke a convincing spirit of a past time. If I read a novel about the Tudor court, I'd like to think it gives a reasonably accurate picture of that court. I quarrel with writers who misrepresent their imagination as history...who purposely set out to give a warped take on the past. Honesty is the key.

Western historian Jim Ronda gives a terse description of bad historical fiction: "Filled with anachronisms, poor sense of place, characters wildly out of type, misunderstanding of the customs and values of a particular time, and the tendency to impose modern standards on the past."

When I asked those gentlemen to define bad historical fiction, I didn't try to lead them by giving them hints of my own convictions on the matter. Now that they have opined so well, my own definition of bad historical fiction hits these points:

- It fails to transport the reader to a former time.
- It fails to put the reader in another place.
- It fails to bring characters to life.

- It fails to make the reader shiver, sweat, sniffle, sneer, snarl, weep, laugh, gag, ache, hunger, wince, yearn, lust, lose sleep, empathize, hate, or need to go potty.
- It seems dubious.
- It has characters who seem too good or too bad to be true.
- It has anachronisms.
- It has clichés and stereotypes.
- Its writing style distracts the reader from the narrative.
- It takes historic license with times and facts.
- It is pointless.
- It is carelessly written.
- It is easy to put down.

That's what a bad historical novel is like. Don't bother writing one like that. Please. There are already thousands out there like that. What I want us all to do is write good historical fiction—enough of us doing it well enough that, like the children in Garrison Keillor's Lake Wobegon, we'll all be above average.

Here are some of the ways bad historical fiction gets written. Let's learn how not to commit these four abominations: anachronisms, clichés, bogged-down description, and unnatural dialogue.

ANACHRONISMS

In a very successful and generally readable novel based on the life of the famous Shoshone Indian interpreter Sacagawea, that only female in Lewis and Clark's company of soldiers took off her clothes to get into the soothing waters of a hot spring on the Lolo Trail. As the author put it, Sacagawea didn't have a "Victorian attitude."

Well, I should think not. There was no such thing as a Victorian attitude yet at that time. The English queen who gave prudishness her name hadn't even been born yet. A historian could make that remark about the Victorian attitude and get away with it, because a historian is looking back from a time when Victoria *has* existed and we know what her attitude was. But in that novel, the consciousness, the point of view, are supposed to be in the year 1804, so the name Victoria should be meaningless to the reader. The author jolts the reader's sense of time travel by mentioning Victoria. The reader *does* know what the allusion means, but isn't *supposed* to know that yet. So the author committed an anachronism: She put an idea out of its chronological place.

Fiction takes the skeleton of historical fact and, without changing that structure, adds flesh, muscle, organs, and most of all, the breath of spirit.

—Dayton Duncan

That's not the same kind of anachronism as a screenwriter once committed by writing, "Tecumseh draws his revolver." That was in a screenplay adaptation of my novel *Panther in the Sky*. By saying "Tecumseh draws his pistol," the screenwriter could have been correct, as the warrior did have pistols, but the type of pistol we call a revolver wasn't yet in use. Tonto might have drawn a revolver, but not Tecumseh.

Speaking of Tecumseh: Sometimes when I'm talking about that Shawnee hero, I describe him as being "as fit and muscular as an Olympic-class athlete." That isn't an anachronism if I say it in a lecture or in nonfiction writing. But would it be an anachronism if I said it in a novel, when I, along with my readers, am back in the early nineteenth century with Tecumseh?

Oddly, the answer could be yes or no. Technically, it wouldn't be an anachronism; there *had* already been Olympic athletes in Greece long before Tecumseh's time. But Tecumseh and the people around him in the novel probably knew nothing about the Ancient Greek Olympic games, so it's unlikely the comparison would be used.

Avoiding anachronisms is almost an art in itself. The historical novelist has to have ways of determining when any particular weapon, tool, procedure, name, idea, or word usage came into being. Anachronisms are traps strewn along the path that runs between Then and Now, and it is easy to fall into them. Avoiding them is one thing editors are for, of course, but it's the author's responsibility not to introduce them in the first place.

I was once saved from an embarrassing anachronism by my keen editor at Random House/Ballantine, the late Pamela Strickler. Ms. Strickler could be a stickler. The protagonist in one of my novels, a man who would have been likely to quote from the Bible, feared in 1778 that the enemy force would, "like the Assyrian, come down like the wolf on the fold," and he thought it in those words. Pam marked in the margin: *anachronism?* So I looked in Bartlett's Quotations. The phrase *wasn't* from the Bible, as I'd thought. It was from a poem that Lord Byron hadn't yet written because he was still unborn in 1778. If my editor hadn't caught that, some nitpicking reader would have. No doubt she kept me from making other anachronisms besides that one, but that example I still squirm to remember.

Use a dictionary—like *Webster's Encyclopedic Unabridged*—or other reference that cites the approximate year when words or terms came into usage, and use Bartlett's for phrases that seem familiar.

A historical novelist often must write about plagues, medical treatments, surgical, birth, bleeding, and medication procedures. Finding out which procedures were in use at a given time requires creative research. Both my parents were physicians, but I didn't inherit their medical school education, so I have to look things up.

I did inherit some of their medical books, which told something about who knew what, and when they knew it. One of my historical characters spent that famously terrible winter at Valley Forge, and I learned that a sip of vinegar was part of a soldier's ration, both to add some tang to the rice or gruel diet and to prevent scurvy. I learned about the ringworm and other awful skin conditions that grew during their months in that bathless environment. And I discovered that one of George Washington's medical officers experimented with live cowpox to inoculate against smallpox that year, which was earlier than I'd thought. That officer's name was Albigence Waldo, and it would have been worth the research just to find a name like that, even if he hadn't been a pioneer in smallpox treatment. Elsewhere, while writing about treating smallpox victims in another novel, I ran across that "tobacco smoke enema" that I mentioned earlier. Medical history can be just wonderfully disgusting. For example, some battlefield surgeons in the 1800s left flesh wounds uncovered so that flies could get on them, because they'd noticed that their maggots eat the rotten flesh away and leave the healthy part.

Back in the 1970s when I was just getting into historical research, a neighbor of mine told me he had something that might interest me. He had bought a new set of *Encyclopedia Britannica* for his library, and as a bonus he'd received a replica of the first set of the Britannica: the three bound volumes originally published beginning in 1769. He gave them to me, and I quickly saw that it was a wonderful anti-anachronism kit. It showed me the "state-of-the-art" knowledge of most arts, sciences, occupations, and philosophies of that time. (Note: the term "state-of-the-art" hadn't yet been coined then. If the paragraph I'm writing now were in a novel, the term would be an anachronism.)

In those keepsake *Britannicas* I could look up what Englishmen knew (or believed) about medicine or astronomy or physics and mathematics or architecture or warfare or almost anything, at just about the time I was depicting. Some of the knowledge in Britannica might not have reached America by that time, but most of it would have. In fact, because of famous colonial intellectuals like Franklin and Jefferson, Americans might have been ahead of some of the stuff in that first Britannica. That could be determined separately, but the old volumes were a windfall for me in those pre-Google, pre-Wikipedia days. (In fact, they still are, because I still don't browse the Internet.)

HOW MANY CLICHÉS CAN STAND ON THE HEAD OF A PIN?

I was sitting in a theater once with a college pal during a performance of *Hamlet*. We heard the actors declaim: "Neither a borrower, nor a lender be," and "Something is rotten in the state of Denmark," and "Though this be madness, yet there is method in 't." When Hamlet finally said, "To be, or not to be: that is the question," my friend's elbow nudged me, and his whisper hissed: "Clichés! Nothing but clichés!"

That was the only time I ever laughed aloud in a performance of *Hamlet*, and it wasn't where Shakespeare meant me to.

The Bard coined more clichés than any other writer. Second place goes to the Spanish novelist Cervantes. (Coincidentally, those two literary giants, who never met, died on the very same day, a meaningless but wistful piece of trivia, the sort that turns up during research.) Third place in international cliché-writing would probably have to go to that busy fellow, Anonymous. They weren't clichés when they were coined. They became clichés because they were so good that everybody kept repeating them.

AS OTHERS SEE IT

Your historical novel is finished, bought up eagerly by a major publishing house, and going into production. Congratulations. No chance of getting disappointed by a rejection slip now!

But brace yourself for one more disappointment: The dust-jacket art.

When the publisher's art department sends you their initial cover picture, your first cry will be: "Didn't they even read the book?" Well, even if they did, their mental picture probably won't match the one you formed in your mind's eye in the months you were researching and writing the novel.

For one thing, the artists probably don't know things you know from all your research. The artists do some research—on costumes, etc.—and they might have done other covers from your time period. But there surely will be things you don't like. You can advise them and argue with them (through your editor, most likely), but you have to accept two facts:

1. They have their own creative imaginations. (Like the movie-makers in chapter 5.)
2. Their marching orders are to create cover art that will make the book fly off the shelves, and they're trained in that art.

I'm not terribly hard to please, but I've had to grit my teeth to accept almost every cover ever done for my books. My complaints have ranged from the image of the protagonist (too hunky a hero, too starlet-like a heroine); landscapes (has that artist never even been outdoors to see that Eastern mountains are hardwood-forested, not piney and craggy like the Rockies?); equipment (that covered wagon would be pulled by oxen, not racehorses); weapons ("The damned Bowie Knife hadn't been designed yet!"); clothing ("Oh, no! Not another coonskin cap!"); and beasts ("Is that a horse, or a saddled dog?").

So I just grumble and go on believing that if the dust-jacket artists had seen things my way, those books would have sold twice as well.

"Anybody who uses clichés should have his head examined," my brother liked to say.

Clichés in prose can be useful, but they're mostly a sign that the author is lazy. And if you the author have your character *deliberately* utter a cliché sometime, make sure it was indeed a cliché by then, lest you make it an anachronism instead.

We usually think of a cliché as being verbal: a trite phrase or expression. Its material form is the stereotype. It stands out in your prose like a sore thumb (if I may use a cliché). Discriminating readers yawn when they see it in a book, and then they shut the book. People who haven't read much might not recognize clichés and stereotypes, might even like them on first reading, but the more they read, the more discriminating they become. So don't introduce a character by describing him as "common as an old shoe." Compare by some things other than by "apples and oranges." Don't have Daniel Boone saying, "We aren't out of the woods yet," unless he's literally in the woods.

And to jump from cliché to stereotype without leaving Daniel Boone: If he appears in one of your novels, describe his headgear as something other than a coonskin cap, will you?

When your villain shows up, don't immediately show him sneering and twirling the end of his mustache. Let your readers discern on their own that he's the villain by watching what he does during the plot. A villain might even be mistaken for a good guy at first; that deception usually gives him better chances to do his evil.

Clichés and stereotypes are shortcuts past creative writing. So many thousands of stories have been written that you're not likely to come up with anything that hasn't been done before. But what you write should be original *as far as you know*. Creative writing means not using what you've seen others write, but being original in every sentence you write.

You should want your writing style to originate and grow out of the bright flashes in your own head, and from your own personal joy and skill in the language.

HOW NOT TO DESCRIBE

Much of your writing style will be shaped by your skill at description. Describing is of crucial importance in historical fiction because, as I've said over and over, you need to put your reader so deep in the center of Then and There that they become Here and Now. Here are some tips on writing description:

Don't use adverbs to embellish weak verbs and adjectives. Rummage in your vocabulary until you find precisely the best word. If it isn't in your vocabulary, obtain it, and use it. Adverbs often end in -*ly,* as in, "His was a disdainfully ironic sense of humor," is better said simply, "he had a wry wit."

Don't stop the narrative and put it "on hold" while you're describing. That's like stopping your car every time you want to glance at scenery or check the rearview mirror. You can describe as you go along, if you use the exact nouns, verbs, and adjectives. That's because they are efficient, and make quick, precise imagery.

For example, you can convey the "mountainness" of a mountain better by having your character climb it than by having him stand and look at it all day.

Same with bodice-ripping and passionate desire. You don't have to stop the action and hover there describing the size, shape, and complexion of a breast your protagonist wants to kiss; that's just voyeurism. Get him right onto it with all his other senses: smell, touch, taste—even sound (heavy breathing, perhaps, or maybe singing *sotto voce* that oldie, "Thanks for the Mammary ...").

Describe vividly. But do it in few words, and keep moving.

UNNATURAL DIALOGUE

Make dialogue "earworthy"!

Dialogue isn't just words and information, it's among those *sounds* that I spoke of in chapter 11. The reader's "mental ear" hears dialogue while the eyes are reading it on the page, and it has to sound like people talking.

In the days when novelist Ayn Rand was a "must-read" for university students and budding tycoons, I gave her books a valiant try, but came to suspect that she wrote her dialogue by putting quotation marks around all her college term papers and political tracts. Her terrible example helped teach me something about dialogue: one way *not* to write it.

Don't, *please* don't, use dialogue just to convey description to the reader. In writing workshops I see so many manuscripts in which the dialogue sounds unnatural because the author is using conversation as a vehicle to reel off descriptions or explanations that he wants the reader to know. For example, dialogue like this:

"Look. This room we're in has beautiful murals!"

"Yes! And here comes the princess, wearing a gown of shimmering silk, the color of apricots!"

What's wrong with that? Simple: Why would people need to describe for each other something that they're both looking at?

Or, even worse: "Welcome, Rodrigo, you broad-shouldered, lithe, black-haired fellow with a sardonically-lifted eyebrow!" That's an outrageous example. But I've read worse.

Dialogue is to be heard. To make it sound natural, read it aloud to yourself, or tape record it and play it back to yourself. Even better, let someone else hear it and tell you whether it sounds real.

And to stay tuned to what dialogue really sounds like, listen to real people talking. Eavesdrop, even; that can be a form of research. Listen not only to the words they say, but to the rhythm of their statements, questions, replies. Sometimes in your novel you might have two people who are really trying to have a dialogue. Sometimes, on the other hand, you'll have two characters talking at each other but determined not to listen. Sometimes a "dialogue" is actually a pair of monologues. That's the way it is in real life, and only if you practice the art of listening can you learn how discourse really works.

Then you'll be prepared to write dialogue that sounds real to your reader's mental ear.

....

You should want your writing style to originate and grow out of the bright flashes in your own head, and from your own personal joy and skill in the language.

....

YE OLD DISCOURSE

As for dialogue of a different and past time, it requires both research and imagination. People in various regions used different words, phrases, and idioms at different times. Many dialects still carry traces of brogues and burrs generations later, as, for example, the old Scots in Appalachia, New England Irish, etc., and keep some of the colloquialisms.

Writers often are tempted to convey the sounds of such speech peculiarities by using what is called "eye dialect." That is, by trying to make the reader hear it the way it looks on the page. You've seen it. It looks like this, as, say, the Clampetts arriving in Beverly Hills: "Wal, hyar we-uns is! Whatcha thank o' this year place?"

Eye dialect has been done by writers for a long time, and sometimes it serves a good purpose. Robert Burns the Scottish poet, could write and spell in perfectly good English, but when he intended to make his English readers hear how Highlanders sounded, as, for example, when addressing a mouse, he used eye dialect: "Wee, sleekit, cow'rin, tim'rous beastie, O, what a panic's in thy breastie! Thou need na start awa sae hasty ..."

(Wouldn't that have played hell with his spell check!)

Sir Harry Lauder, later, wrote songs that tried even harder to look, on paper, the way Scottish speech sounds: "It's a braw brecht moonlecht necht, / Yer a' recht, that's a'." Without the eye dialect, that would be, "It's a brave bright moonlight night, /You're all right, that's all."

Late nineteenth-century America had Joel Chandler Harris, creator of old Uncle Remus, who was later made famous by Walt Disney in Song of the South. Harris's eye dialect became the model for just about anyone who wanted to write African American–sounding dialect, whether to charm the reader or ridicule the blacks: "Youk'n hide de fier, but w'at you gwine do wid de smoke?"

Or, for the Irish, Finley Peter Dunne's "Mr. Dooley" sketches: "Th' dead ar-re always pop'lar. I knowed a society wanst to vote a monyment to a man an' refuse to help his fam'ly, all in wan night."

Got a French Canadian in your story? "Sacre bleu! Vair deed you poot ze canoe pad–dell, M'syoo?"

Much such eye-dialect writing was done early in the twentieth century, and never really died out. Wanting the reader to know it's someone with an accent or dialect speaking, the author tries to use that device. If you've got an Australian or an English limey in your story, you want the reader to be aware of it. So you go to work with apostrophes and contrived misspellings.

Eye dialect is tempting, but it isn't that good an idea. You have to be awfully good at it to make the reader enjoy it, and even then it can be more distraction than it's worth. The better way to convey foreign or regional speech is by researching in colloquialism, to learn the idioms and speech patterns of other places and other times.

That's a field of research in itself. Like much other research for historical writing, it raises the question: "So what? What reader is going to know or care whether the hero's mother would call the evening meal 'dinner' or 'supper?'" The answer is, "Some reader will." A cherished example:

An elderly reader hurried up to me at a library event in Appalachian Kentucky, and, her eyes a-twinkle, pointed to an opened page of my novel and exclaimed, "When this lady come out on the porch and yelled out 'Supper's on the board!' I knew the author knew us folks! 'Cause that's just what my Gran'ma always did holler to get the men folk in to eat!"

"Not, 'Soooo-EEE'?"

She grinned and slapped my wrist. "No, hon, *that's* for callin' them *other* pigs!"

AND, FINALLY ...

Always double-, triple-, quadruple-check your prose to be sure you haven't gotten carried away by the action and written sentences like these that I've found in manuscripts:

"He saw Cherokee warriors coming out of the corner of his eye." (That must have been on the Trail of Tears.)

And my favorite stereotypical true-grit frontier woman image:

"With her left hand she held the baby to one breast while shooting at Indians with the other."

A vivid image, indeed, but surely not what the writer meant.

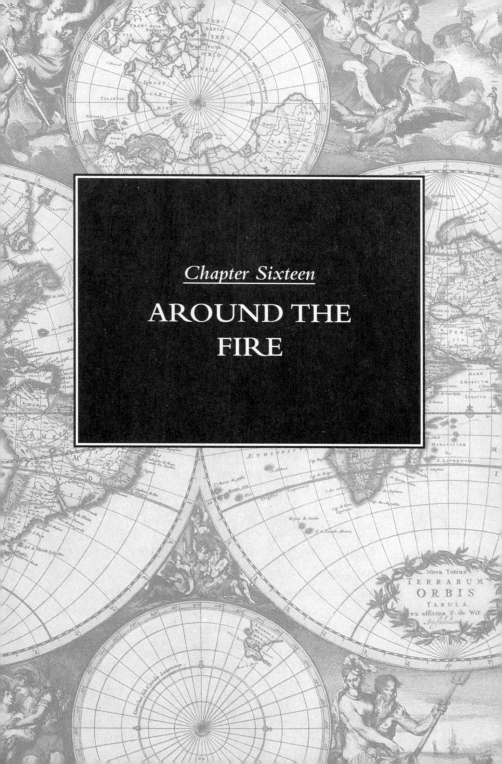

Chapter Sixteen

AROUND THE
FIRE

aving spent my adult life thinking of, traveling in, and writing about the dimension of Time, I've come to believe that everything that makes up humanity and human civilization began as storytelling.

And for much of human existence, all that storytelling was done around a fire.

Man surely separated himself from the other animals when he became conscious of his consciousness: when he realized that he was thinking. At that time, as it was put so poetically by the great scientific writer Loren Eiseley, man stepped out through a leafy curtain, and the foliage closed behind him.

And we have never been able to find our way back through. We're lonely for the animals we were before we emerged through the curtain. So we turned our faces toward fire, and found that it dispelled the loneliness.

Ever since, on the banks of the long River of Time, we have huddled together around campfires, cookfires, hearthfires, looking across the firelight at each other and trying to express this humanness in which we find ourselves.

Imagine yourself as your earliest and most primitive ancestor. Your name might be Grok or Moomah, or it might be Adam or Eve. You wander alone in daylight through a wilderness of forms and stimuli that are nameless—because you don't really have a language yet—looking for food, looking for a mate. In those ways, you're still like the other animals. You're learning through your senses and instincts what is good to eat, what is comfortable, what stings or bites, what pleases the eye or the ear, what makes you salivate, what makes you yearn to mate. You hear wind in the trees, birdsong, trickling water, thunder, the rustle or growl of an animal in the grass. You smell a flower, a rotting carcass, rain-freshened air, smoke, the estrus of a female. Feelings stir and change inside you. Fear. Belly-hunger, other hungers. An itch, or many itches. Unlike the other earthbound mammals, you might yearn to rise and be up where you see a hawk soaring.

When night falls, you join your family in the cave or under some sheltering roof you've made, and there is a fire in the center. You are unlike the other animals in that you use fire, and you gather around it with your family, your pack of kin. You look around at them, and you have an urge: You want to share what you learned or observed or wondered about out there in the woods and fields today. In other words: You have a story to tell.

You can mime. But you'll need words. You'll need names for things. You can't tell a story until you have a language.

And so it begins.

Hunters tell how they succeeded in catching and killing an elusive prey. Gatherers tell of finding a way to collect a particular kind of grain kernel in great quantities. Such food-getting tales told around the fire become the information that we now would call their "economy."

Women find that willow bark can make an ache go away, or that bear grease protects their skin from bug bites and sunburn, or that the mashed leaves of a certain plant can be held on a wound to ease pain. Such stories become "medicine." Men complain of other men's behavior, say they should be made to act better, and those stories become rules for coexistence, and thus "law" begins to evolve. Families boast of the strength and wisdom of their fathers and grandfathers, and "history" is invented. Tribes from beyond the mountain describe what was there: "geography." Someone imitates a birdcall, and there is the beginning of "music." The music stirs someone to move gracefully, and there is "dance." A baby pees on his grandfather's knees, somebody imitates an ape, the others laugh, and "comedy" is born.

People try to comprehend what they hear in the wind, see in lightning or the sun and stars and the changing shape of the moon, what they sense in birth and death, and when they realize that some Great Something pervades the material world and makes life, they give it a name that means "God," and religion enters into their being. Likewise, "philosophy," and "ethics," and "trade," or any belief or system by which we function.

And the stories themselves, by which all these civilizing categories began, they were told over and over, and new ones entered the repertoire, and "literature" was under way, which meant there would eventually be a need for "writers," which brings us to that topic of keenest interest: ourselves.

That's why I say that storytelling is the origin of everything meaningful to the human race and that it all began and developed around a fire in the center.

Fire itself has been an inspirational or legendary spirit; it has been deemed a gift from the Creator, to help man survive. Sun-worshipping cultures believed that fire was a tiny bit of the sun, seized and used by Man, but not by the other animals, to help sustain us in winter and night. Most cultures have a version of that legend, probably composed under the inspiration of the hearth fire itself, and told as the storyteller's eyes gleamed in firelight.

Many an early philosopher or scientist tried to understand whether fire was itself a form of life. Why not? It's born in a spark, it grows, it eats, it changes its food (fuel) into waste, it starves and dies if not fed, it talks to us, it helps us as a friend helps us, but can turn into a destroying enemy.

To many ancients, fire was not just alive, it was sacred. Most modern Indians have to instruct their guests not to throw cigarette butts, wrappers, or any other trash in the campfire, or to spit in it, or extinguish it by peeing on it, as beer-drinking campers like to do.

In Greek mythology, the Titan Prometheus stole fire from the gods and made a gift of it to man. In the Lenni Lenape (Delaware) Indian story, all the two-legged human people were freezing to death in winter darkness, until M'Noukahaszh, the Crow, the bird with the sweetest song and the most colorful plumage, volunteered to fly to heaven and ask Creator for sunlight for the people. Creator was annoyed by the two-leggeds and wouldn't give them sunlight. So, Crow stole a stick, lit it from the sun, and fled toward earth with it. And thus it was Crow who brought man that indispensable gift, but in his long dive back to earth with the burning brand in his beak, his gorgeous feathers were blackened and his melodious voice was made hoarse by the soot and smoke from the burning stick. As the saying goes, "No good deed goes unpunished." Likewise, in the stories of other aboriginal peoples, fire is brought from the sky by a thunderbird, perhaps reflecting their observation that prairie and forest fires often followed lightning storms.

In the old days before matches and cigarette lighters, fires were hard to start, so certain persons were designated firekeepers, with responsibility to keep tribal fires from dying out. Nomadic and hunting peoples devised painstaking ways to carry fire from place to place.

Readers of Jean Auel's prehistory novels may remember the resourceful heroine, Ayla, carrying the fire. That series, beginning with *The Clan of the Cave Bear*, was a remarkably successful example of what can be done with imaginative historical fiction, conveying a scope much greater than the basic narrative, as I've said a good historical novel should do.

Auel worked not so much with reference to the work of history scholars, but with reference to the studies of anthropologists, paleontologists, zoologists, and other scientists, to determine when humans began doing what, and how. She wrote of those ancient times vividly, imagining how preliterate peoples learned and evolved in that long, dangerous journey of survival. Her work shows us that historical fiction (or, in that case, prehistorical fiction) can go anywhere in time, take the reader into unexpected places, and teach significant lessons even about our very origins.

The only strain she puts upon verisimilitude, in my opinion, is that her protagonist personally comes up with virtually all the innovations that in actuality would have been developed and discovered by countless primitive men and women over many generations. In that regard, Ayla is a prototype, a titan, standing as an analogue of mankind's early progress. Most titan guys were famous for just one deed.

....

[W]hen I gaze into a fire, I feel connected to all the people who have been looking down into flames and up at soaring sparks for hundreds of thousands of years, telling or listening to the stories by which we've become human civilizations.

....

But Ayla was woman. And as we know from clichés, woman's work is never done.

Other prehistory novels have been researched and written well, such as the mammoth-hunting books by a husband-and-wife writing couple, Kathleen and Michael Gear, and the Eskimo novels by Sue Harrison. For all their remoteness in the distant past, they are exciting, dramatic, and very human, and they teach by putting the reader "way back when."

For even at the dawn of humanity, once upon a time it was now, and an educated imagination can put you there and get you started telling a story.

Do keep in mind that from then onward, through hundreds of thousands of years, any story will be warmed and lit in the center

INSPIRATION IS CONTAGIOUS

One of the truest statements I ever read came from Horace Walpole, an 18th Century English writer: "This world is a comedy to those that think, a tragedy to those that feel."

Since most of us both think and feel, what we see in the world affects us both ways, at different times. The same event can make us feel amused or poignant. Whichever, it inspires us to some emotional response, and enough intellectual response that we consider the meaning of it.

I've said that happy endings are rare in life, and realistic storytelling usually ends otherwise. But both comedy and tragedy can inspire, if the end result is a lifting and broadening of the human spirit—if the reader comes away with some admiration for the protagonist. Readers tell me they might forget my name or the exact title of a book of mine, but they never forget the heroes and heroines who go through hell and come out dignified, strengthened, and above bitterness. Over the decades of my writing life, I've learned that the most important thing I give my readers is not mere information, or entertainment, but inspiration.

Of course, it's inspiration that motivates me to tell the stories in the first place, so what I'm doing as a storyteller is simply passing on the inspiration. Eventually, though, I printed on a sticky note in big letters my new motto—INSPIRATION IS CONTAGIOUS—and I stuck it on my wall above Abraham Lincoln's portrait.

by fire. Until the invention of furnaces and electric heat, geothermal and flameless heat pumps, families had fire as their intimate and essential home companion, arguably rivaling the dog himself as man's best friend. Remember that you can't tell history well without the sight, sound, smell, and feel of living fire, as well as the change that cooking made in food. Fire is perceived by all the five senses, and it's evocative to the "sixth sense." A writer could hardly ask more of any single thing.

But after all the ages with fire in the center of the story, with the River of Time flowing by, the light is changing: Now the light in the center of the home, gleaming in the eyes of the family members, the light by which we get our stories, is no longer fire. It's electronic. It's the television or computer screen. Or it's several of them, one in each family member's room. Each family member focuses on a different aspect of the culture: one on video games, maybe, one on a football game, one on a NASCAR race, one on *American Idol*, one on a chat room, another on MySpace. With the fire gone, the family conscious is dispersed. The light before their eyes isn't drawing them together; it's drawing them apart. The old family history seems boring and pointless, because, as that one girl told her mother back in chapter 1, "I'm not in it."

This might seem normal and okay to the very young. But to those of us who have sat telling and listening to stories by the fireplace or around a campfire, it's sad and disturbing.

One of my earliest memories is of lying prone on a rug in front of the fireplace, my sister and one of my brothers beside me. Each of us had a pencil and some paper that our parents had given us, and we were making up stories and drawing pictures to illustrate them. That night was more than 70 years ago. I can still feel the heat on my face. The most recent time I sat in front of a fireplace and told a story was last night. Some visitors had asked me where I got the unusual red granite stones I built my fireplace with, and I told them a story: Those stones had originally been quarried by prison convicts and used as the cobblestone floor of the train station in St. Louis. I first walked on them when my grandmother and I got off of a passenger train there before World War II. The second time I saw those stones I was on a trainload of Marine recruits heading west to get on a ship to Korea. The third time I saw them, I was taking a train trip from Indianapolis to Mexico City.

The fourth time I saw those stones, tons of them were piled in the yard of a stone company near here. I learned that the old St. Louis train station had been gutted and made over into a fancy urban shopping mall, and these stones had been removed and sold by the trainload to stone dealers all over the country. I was fifty years old by then and was building this log cabin, and so I bought a few tons of them and used them on the fireplace. They were, as you see, loaded with stories for me, and I continue to add stories and memories to them every time I build a fire in there to reminisce by with my friends and colleagues.

We still watch fire, not television. We can see anything we want to see in a fire. At all other ages of my life I've watched hearth fires and campfires, at church camps, beside canoeing rivers, on beaches, on mountains, in deserts, in caves, on research treks, in tepees, at Indian powwows and sweat-lodge ceremonies, in re-enactor encampments, on honeymoon nights, in state and national parks (in varying degrees of sobriety). And when I gaze into a fire, I feel connected to all the people who have been looking down into flames and up at soaring sparks for hundreds of thousands of years, telling or listening to the stories by which we've become human civilizations.

The storyteller's fire is older and more constant than even the Eternal Flame that burns at the Tomb of the Unknown Soldier in Paris. And whoever that unknown soldier was, we can be pretty sure that he, as he was growing up to become a corpse on a battlefield, learned much of what he knew and believed by looking into a fireplace with his family, or a campfire with his comrades-in-arms. Everything is story, and it should always be by firelight.

If anyone I've ever known sat at as many fires telling and hearing stories as I have, I'd guess that would have been Stephen Ambrose, the historian whose remark one day out West provoked me to articulate the ideas that make this book. I know that man was a lifelong campfire storyteller. Although I never sat at a campfire with him on the banks of the Missouri River, I sat by campfires in many of the same places, just at different times.

Stephen, as I said, passed away before the observation of the Lewis and Clark Bicentennial he'd promoted so eloquently. He was gone before I had a chance to ask him the questions I asked other historians for this book. I didn't get to ask him if he really was all that contemptuous of novelists. I didn't get to ask him whether he had ever thought of writing a novel himself.

But recently I did ask his daughter, Stephenie. My wife and I came to know and love her during the bicentennial years, appearing with her on lecture programs, C-SPAN panels, and the like, and I was comfortable with the idea of interviewing her father through her.

I asked her how he might have defined "good" historical fiction, or whether he thought there even is such a thing. I'd gotten the impression that he didn't think there was. "Did he ever express such opinions to you?" I asked.

He hadn't actually given such opinions, not that she remembered. She did relate some things, though, that revealed in him the kind of neck-deep activity, emotional involvement and imagination that a novelist needs. She told about those annual family canoe and boat trips on the Missouri. Those nights around the campfire, where he would read aloud the journal entries the explorers and their men wrote on those specific days in those specific campsites almost two centuries before, his gruff voice tight with emotion and wonderment.

He got that involved in all his research and storytelling. Like my own father, he had taken all his children to Gettysburg Battlefield. She said, "He gave us each a stick, and we pretended they were muskets. Then he told us about the Union defense of Little Round Top. And then he gave a yell and we all charged toward the hill. We were there! He made us live that day!"

Aha! The famous no-nonsense historian in a historical reenactment! That made me feel good. I asked, "Did he ever say he'd like to write historical fiction?" She said: "Dad did write a novel."

He had written it years before, then put it away. It told the life story of George Shannon, youngest member of the Lewis and Clark party, who lived a long and distinguished life beyond the great adventure. When Ambrose knew his time was running out, a publisher asked him if he had any as yet unpublished manuscripts. Stephen's wife Moira remembered where the manuscript was stored away, and out it came.

It's written in the form of Shannon's imaginary diary. Its title is a phrase from the real Lewis and Clark journals: *This Vast Land*. Thorndike Press published it posthumously.

Being a novel, it is, of course, fiction.

But its author, being a historian, had to know facts.

I'm happy to know that Stephen Ambrose got around to writing a historical novel while he was alive. It's fitting that a man who told stories over that many campfires should write at least one novel.

THE FIRE INSIDE

As men and women through the millennia gathered around the fires and told the stories, almost every one of them must have thought, at least once: I am a fire, myself!

Most of us understand intuitively that to be alive is to burn. We are warm because we are burning the fuel we call food. If our lives are good, we will give off some light that will guide our offspring. If our lives are bad, our fire might burn down things and blacken other lives. And in the end each life will die out and leave its ashes, but the fire, the spirit, will have ignited the next generation, which then will ignite the next.

Whether a character in your novel is full of choler, bile, phlegm, blood, or plain old buffalo chips, the fire of life is in there, too, as long as that character lives.

Fire might appear in your novel in many dramatic forms—campfire, smoke signals, a whale oil lamp, an oven, a volcano, a burning house or a burning ship, in the heating of water for a childbirth or of iron for sword-making, in lethal gunfire, in a vicious arson, in the burning of an enemy fort, or of Atlanta, for that matter, in the cauterizing of wounds from a battle, in a duel or a fratricide, or, at last, the cremation of the corpse.

WORDS FROM FIRE

But the most dramatic single thing that ever happened by firelight didn't happen in a flash. It was slow, oh, so slow. It had to happen first, so that the storytelling could begin.

I mean the growth and nurturing of language. You must give thought to this miracle.

It must have taken countless frustrating years for those earliest people around the campfires to build the vocabularies and forms of speech with which to tell the stories, to express the wonderment, to build oratory by which to persuade and lead. If you've never thought of the miracle of language, well, damn it, start thinking about it!

It's what we all live by, not just writers. All languages are intricate, beautiful, rich, old, and new. The one I'm using here, English, is probably the most effective and evocative of all. Certain outstanding writers who began in their native languages—Conrad in Polish, Nabokov in Russian, for two examples—adopted English because they could do so much more with it.

Whether a character in your novel is full of choler, bile, phlegm, blood, or plain old buffalo chips, the fire of life is in there, too, as long as that character lives.

Language itself is like fire, enriching and enlightening our lives, forever changing.

I mean, dude, language is, like, you know, awesome!

Duh! (Grunt.)

Our ancestors gave us a great language. You as a storyteller must strive to be worthy of it.

If you aren't in awe of language, if you take it for granted, if you hope to get through life with a minimum knowledge of it, if you're lazy and sloppy with it, then you aren't fit to be a storyteller, a historian, a novelist, a teacher, or even a parent. If you need to express something important, but instead just shrug and mutter, "Whatever," you don't even deserve a place in this long, beautiful, ghastly, and poignant stream of stories that was, is, and forever will be the human tale, the one which begins:

Once upon a time …

THE END

INDEX

ACKNOWLEDGEMENTS

Many of the people who helped me conceive and create this book are dead. Some were dead even before they helped me. Nevertheless, they deserve credit for what this book has become.

Stephen Ambrose, celebrated American historian, helped me without even knowing it, and died before I could thank him. He would've thought my thanks were facetious anyway, probably.

Other dead persons who influenced this book are Mark Twain, Teddy Roosevelt, Marine Gen. Smedley Butler, and the vainglorious cavalryman George Custer, who died, as we know, by committing Siouxicide. They all helped me understand how faint and flimsy the line is between history and historical fiction.

The late Dr. Werner Beyer, my creative writing professor at Butler University, half a century ago gave me the single storytelling tip that has best helped me succeed in this business. Loren Eiseley, paleontologist and poet, mentored me in the art of thinking beyond the skull. Historian Howard Zinn helped me keep "glory" in perspective.

Then there are all those old dead soldiers named Thom and whalers named Swain who prepared for me the sense of my place in the flow of American history.

I owe thanks to these who are still living: historians Dayton Duncan, James Ronda, John Sugden, Lanford Jones, James Holmberg, and Stephenie Ambrose Tubbs; and novelists Sharyn McCrumb and Lucia St. Clair Robson.

The editor who first accepted my idea for this book, then guided me through to its completion, is Lauren Mosko. She patiently helped this old quillpusher overcome cyberphobia and write on a computer for the first time.

Finally, I thank my wife Dark Rain, not just for her pertinent chapter on genealogical research, but for her wisdom, her steady moral support, and her ability to spring to the computer keyboard and retrieve paragraphs or whole chapters that my clumsy fingers had zapped off into cyberspace.

Any failings of this book are, of course, the computer's fault.

ABOUT THE AUTHOR

James Alexander Thom believes that the way to understand history is to "be in it when it's happening." Readers of his nine deeply-researched American frontier books consistently respond with the words he loves to hear: "I felt like I was there!"

Ranging from Colonial Virginia to the conquest of the West, his prize-winning epics have sold 2.5 million copies and are assigned as supplemental reading in history courses by teachers who trust the history in the tales. He shows the Indian Wars through the eyes and souls of both whites and Native Americans.

He has been awarded literature prizes and a Doctorate of Humane Letters for his lifetime writing accomplishments, and presented with eagle feathers and blankets by American Indian leaders for his telling of their peoples' history.

An Indiana-born Marine Corps veteran, former metropolitan newspaperman and Indiana University Journalism School lecturer, he lives with his Shawnee Indian wife, Dark Rain, in the wooded Southern Indiana hills, in a log house he erected using pioneer tools and techniques. He is a sculptor and an illustrator.